Richard W. Seelan
Carmel, California
January 16, 1981

THE BIRD YEAR
A BOOK FOR BIRDERS
With Special Reference to the Monterey Bay Area

by
John Davis

Research Zoologist, Museum of Vertebrate Zoology
University of California (Berkeley)
In charge of Hastings Natural History Reservation
Carmel Valley, California

and
Alan Baldridge

Hopkins Marine Station
of Stanford University
in Pacific Grove, California

THE BOXWOOD PRESS

ISBN: 0-910286-62-0

Distributed
by
The Boxwood Press
183 Ocean View Blvd.
Pacific Grove, CA 93950

Cover photograph
by
Ben Lyon
Monterey Peninsula Herald

Printed in U.S.A.

PREFACE

THE INCEPTION of this book was a suggestion made to our publishers, Ralph and Mildred Buchsbaum, by newspaper publisher (and birder) Paul Block, that there should be a regional guide to the birds of the Monterey Bay area. After we agreed to attempt this, the Buchsbaums and we decided that we should not produce another "what bird is that?" book. Rather, it was felt that it would be more helpful to provide birders with information on the seasonal biology of our birds, what lies behind their annual cycles, and what kinds of habitats they utilize, and what roles they play in the workings of the ecosystem. This book has been, for all of us, something of an experimental venture. We hope that the information presented will make birds even more enjoyable to the birders of the Monterey Bay area, and perhaps elsewhere, by providing some explanations for various aspects of avian biology of which birders have a general awareness without knowing what factors underlie them.

A number of people have helped us in various ways. Ron Branson, Franklin Enos, Frans Lanting and the Monterey Peninsula Herald generously provided most of the photographs which accompany the text. James R. Griffin provided much information on the vegetation of this area. Vern Yadon checked over the lists of birds typical of local habitats and made a number of valuable suggestions. Others who helped us were David Ainley, Dave Bockman, Victoria Dziadosz, Bill Francis, Oxy Hurlbert, Dorothy Lilly, L. Richard Mewaldt, Ferd Ruth, Jocelyn Tyler, and Jud Vandevere.

Finally, we wish to express our thanks to Ralph and Mildred Buchsbaum for their encouragement, advice, and tolerance, which made working with them a real pleasure.

John Davis
Alan Baldridge

Monterey Bay Area
March 1980

CONTENTS

1

INTRODUCTION

THE REMARKABLE RISE in the popularity of birding, or birdwatching, in the past decade has been well described by Small (1974). The keeping of lists of various kinds, the "big day," the seeking out of rarities, and other aspects of this hobby, have provided fine recreation for many people. The participation of birders in the Audubon Society's Christmas Bird Counts has made available a massive body of data which has been put to good use by professional ornithologists. In a paper in *American Birds,* Bock and Lepthien (1974) used computer analysis of 2,743 Christmas Bird Counts to show major patterns of bird species diversity and abundance in the United States and southern Canada in winter. Other authors have used similar data to work out various aspects of avian distribution and population dynamics. The seasonal reports published in *American Birds* provide much detailed information on occurrence.

Yet, birds are among the most highly specialized of animals, and even the commonest, most familiar species show striking adaptations which have evolved in response to the demands of their environments. Merely to record the presence of different kinds of birds, or to census them, is to miss a great deal of fascinating and easily observed natural history.

Every birder is aware that birds have a yearly schedule that varies from species to species, and from place to place. Some birds, such as the Wrentit and the Brown Towhee, reside in a particular area throughout the year and may be found there at any time. Others, such as the Black-headed Grosbeak or the Golden-crowned Sparrow, may occupy a local area for only part of the year. Still others, such as the Northern Phalarope and the Sabine's Gull, may pass through a particular region only at certain times. Conversely, certain months are characterized by the presence of a large variety of species not found at any other time. Birders on the coast of California look forward to the great shorebird migrations of spring and fall, and in the east and midwest the northward passage of countless millions of wood warblers and other songbirds in spring is an eagerly awaited event. Birders are also aware of the seasonality of other aspects of bird biology. For example, in most temperate zone areas, bird song is widespread, and nests are found commonly, only at certain times of the year.

The purpose of this book is twofold. First, we provide information on what lies behind the seasonal, or cyclic, features of bird biology and indicate why certain activities of birds occur at particular times of year. We also give information on how the timing of these events is brought about, and how these various cyclic activities are integrated into a coordinated series which we may call the "annual cycle." Our emphasis in the first part of the book is on seasonal activities and processes such as breeding behavior, reproduction, migration, molting, and the like. We do not discuss such everyday features of bird life as flight, excretion, vision, digestion, and the like, although each and every one of these is, in birds, highly specialized and interesting in its own right. Throughout, we have tried to draw examples from kinds of birds which are familiar to the reader. However, the information presented may be widely applied to most North Temperate Zone species.

In the second part of the book, we describe critically the various bird habitats of the Monterey Bay area, note what species are characteristic of each, and present habitat-related aspects of the biology of some of these species. Although the habitats described are characteristic of the Monterey Bay area, nearly all are of widespread occurrence elsewhere, and much of the information may be used in other areas.

We have given bibliographic references throughout. This is done for three reasons. First, the reader who wishes to explore further will have references to look up. Second, we wish to indicate to all readers the extent, complexity, and varied nature of the literature of ornithology as evidence of how much work has been done on birds. Third, and by no means least, we feel that those who have provided the facts on which this book has been based should be recognized and acknowledged for their contributions.

For the purpose of this book, the area covered is based primarily on the distribution of, and use by, local birders rather than local birds. Our concept of the Monterey Bay area covered extends from Santa Cruz to Big Sur, and from the crests of the Santa Cruz and Santa Lucia mountains west to the pelagic waters beyond the continental shelf. We have also included the drainage of the Carmel River, as it is easily accessible to, and popular with, borders in the Monterey Peninsula area.

In places we have utilized information contained in the field note files of the Hastings Natural History Reservation in the upper Carmel Valley. We have reprinted the "List of the Birds of the Monterey Peninsula Region" in Appendix 2. This list, compiled by the Check-list Committee of the Monterey Peninsula Audubon Society, presents concisely much useful information on the status of many of our birds, and when and where they occur.

2

THE NAMES OF BIRDS

In THE FOLLOWING accounts we shall frequently use bird names, sometimes at the subspecies level, mainly at the species level, rarely at the higher levels of genus, family, and order. These represent increasingly large groups. If one thumbs through Peterson (1961) or Robbins et al (1966), he will get a good "working" idea of the nature of such groups, except for the subspecies. The species category is the most important to the birder, since it refers to a particular kind of bird and is the basis for the life list.

The subspecies, or "geographic race," is a subdivision of the species which has distinctive physical characters and *breeds* in a particular geographic area. For example, the White-crowned Sparrows of our area are represented by three subspecies. The Nuttall's White-crown is a permanent resident of the coastal strip. In the fall it is joined by the Gambel's White-crown and the Puget Sound White-crown; these birds arrive from the north in early fall and leave for northern breeding grounds in early spring. Rarely, as in the case of the White-crowns, subspecies can be identified in the field with some degree of certainty. In the great majority of cases they are distinguished on the basis of subtle color or pattern differences and/or small size differences which may be seen (or measured) only in adequate samples of specimens. Except for the rare subspecies that can be identified with certainty in the field, they should be ignored by birders.

The species has been a problem to birders, as professional ornithologists sometimes eliminate one or more from the list of species which they recognize or, rarely, divide an existing species into two. This has been a source of annoyance and perplexity to many birders, and we feel that it is important that they realize that such changes are not frivolous but are based on important biological principles. We hope that the following discussion will be helpful.

In 1973, *American Birds* carried an article entitled "What the AOU Check-list Committee has done to your life list," by Robert Arbib. The author, noting that "the policy of *American Birds* is to follow current AOU usage," went on to discuss the name changes proposed in the "Thirty-second Supplement to the American Ornithologists' Union Check-list of North American Birds," which appeared in the April 1973 issue of *The Auk*; and he listed those changes involving new status for a number of species. As Arbib pointed out, some changes involved merging two or more former species into one ("lumping"), as exemplified by combining the former Baltimore and Bullock's orioles into a single species, the Northern Oriole. Other changes involved dividing a single species into two species ("splitting"), as exemplified by dividing the Boat-tailed Grackle into the Boat-tailed and Great-tailed grackles. Since most changes in species status involved lumping rather than splitting, birders following current AOU nomenclature lost a number of species from their life lists.

Although Arbib's article was most useful to birders, it did not discuss what lay behind the various lumpings and splittings but referred the reader to the literature references contained in the "Supplement." Many of these references are quite technical and deal with complex situations not easily understood by the non-biologist. However, the principles involved are of great biological significance, and we feel that it is important that birders understand what lies behind changes in species status.

Two major questions are involved in such situations. First, how do we define a distinct species (kind) of bird? Second, how do we decide on the names which we use for species of birds? These questions seem simple and straightforward. The answers are neither.

To begin with, it must be understood that formal, scientific descriptions of new species of birds are based on specimens collected in the field. These are later described by ornithologists working in museums, universities, or, rarely, in privately maintained collections. A specimen usually consists of a stuffed, dried skin, including the appendages (bill, wings, tail, legs, and feet). A label is tied around the legs of each specimen bearing at least the name of the collector, the exact locality and date of collection, and the sex of the specimen as determined by direct examination of the internal organs when this is possible. The professional ornithologist concerned with the classification and naming of bird species can examine only certain external features of the bird from which the skin was made. Pattern and coloration, and the size and shape of the appendages form the primary bases for the description of a new species of bird.

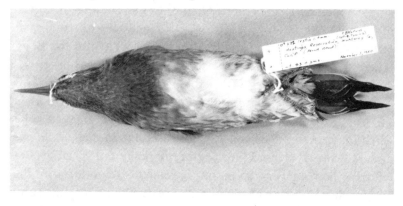

Museum specimen of a red-breasted sapsucker. The appendages are arranged so as to take up the least amount of space in a specimen tray. Pertinent data are on the label attached to the legs. (R. Buchsbaum)

In the 18th and 19th centuries, when most species of birds were described, ornithologists had little interest in the behavior and ecology of the birds which they described. Indeed, many of the most prolific describers of new species did not collect their own specimens but received them from field collectors. They had no first-hand knowledge of the living birds which provided the material they studied. Further, in those early days, when large areas of the New World were just beginning to be explored critically, the emphasis was placed on what kinds of animals were present, and the collecting and/or describing of birds occupied most professional ornithologists.

Under these circumstances, it is not surprising that new species of birds were described primarily on the basis of *how different they appeared* from previously described species. Thus, *degree of difference* was the primary criterion used to decide whether or not the specimens being studied were to be described formally as a new species. This approach to classification ignored the relationships among bird species and the evolutionary considerations involved. Indeed, most species of birds had been described before 1859, when the publication of Charles Darwin's *Origin of Species* introduced the concept of natural selection and put the study of organic evolution on the right track.

This concept of the species persisted well up into the 1920s. For example, Glover Allen, author of *Birds and Their Attributes,* published in 1925 and regarded at the time as the best general text on ornithology available in this country, stated: "A convenient test is that if all the specimens can be referred without doubt to one or the other sort, they are species, as in the case of our Downy and Hairy Woodpeckers."

Our steadily increasing knowledge of the evolutionary process eventually brought about a new concept, *the biological species concept.* One of the first meaningful definitions of an animal species was given by Ernst Mayr (1940): "Species are groups of actually or potentially interbreeding natural populations, which are reproductively isolated from other such groups." Here, we have substituted for "degree of difference" the criterion of *"reproductive isolation."* Individuals which belong to a given species can interbreed freely and produce *fertile* offspring, but they cannot accomplish this with individuals of another species. Therefore, the individuals of a given species are *reproductively isolated* from the individuals of any other species, no matter how closely related.

Regardless of how closely two populations may resemble each other, if they have overlapping distributions *in the breeding season* and do not interbreed, they are considered to be two species. Many of the so-called *"Empidonax"* flycatchers are notoriously difficult to tell apart in the field and occur together in the breeding season in various combinations. Since they do not interbreed they are considered to represent different species.

The cause of reproductive isolation between two very similar species may be the result of physiological incompatibility, which makes the production of fertile offspring impossible; or it may be ecological, with two species, although present in the same restricted breeding area, occupying different habitats; or it may be behavioral, with differences especially in courtship and mating behavior preventing successful reproduction. Mere geographic isolation, as in the case of an island population being cut off by a water barrier from the rest of the species range, is not considered definite proof of reproductive isolation, as in such cases we do not have the opportunity to see how the separated populations would react to each other under natural conditions.

The question is often asked if there is doubt as to the exact relationship between two populations of birds, why not keep mixed pairs in an aviary and see if they interbreed successfully? Unfortunately, little light can be shed on the problem in this manner. Failure to interbreed may well be the result of abnormal conditions, with unnatural diet, lack of sufficient space, absence of proper vegetation, and other departures from the natural situation being enough to discourage mating and successful production of young. Successful interbreeding may simply be the result of restricting a given male or female to the choice of only one or a few mates, or bringing together two individuals that, in nature, might be kept apart by different habitat preferences. Successful reproduction between captive individuals does mean that, at least, they are physiologically compatible, although their offspring would have to be bred to establish fertility. However, this would tell us little about what would happen to the individuals concerned under natural conditions.

An example of a difficult case involves the Scrub Jay and an isolated Florida population of jays that is readily distinguishable from the Scrub Jay in appearance but is generally similar and obviously closely related to it. The question is, *how* closely? Are the Florida birds a distinct species, or should they be considered simply a well-marked population of the Scrub Jay? Since the Florida birds are geographically isolated from the nearest Scrub Jays, in Texas, we do not have the opportunity to see whether or not they would interbreed successfully with the Scrub Jay under natural conditions.

In such cases, we must be careful not to emphasize differences in appearance but balance them against similarities. We must also consider similarities and differences in the ecologies and behaviors of the two populations, since these would be important regarding reproductive isolation. In this particular case, despite consistent and well-marked differences in appearance between Florida birds and the Scrub Jay, there are also many similarities in appearance, structure, ecology, and behavior between them, and the Florida population, once considered a distinct species, should be regarded simply as a well-marked population of the Scrub Jay, Pitelka (1951). The great majority of ornithologists agrees with this conclusion. The decision in this case implies that should the Florida birds and some other population of Scrub Jay ever come into contact naturally, they would interbreed successfully.

Another reason for name changes involves the collection of critical specimens which had been lacking before. A good example of such a case involves the Baltimore and Bullock's orioles. For many years these two readily distinguishable orioles had been considered to represent two species, the Baltimore Oriole occupying the eastern United States and the Bullock's, the western. Occasional hybrids between the two forms had been known for many years but it was not until 1936 that the eminent ornithologist and artist George M. Sutton collected a series of hybrids between the two forms where their ranges met in Oklahoma and described and illustrated them (Sutton, 1938). By 1957, it was realized that these two "species" hybridized extensively in Nebraska and Oklahoma.

Sibley and Short (1964) analyzed in detail the nature of variation in 634 specimens of adult orioles (602 males, 32 females) collected in the Great Plains. They demonstrated clearly that the Baltimore and Bullock's orioles hybridize along a zone 160-240 km wide extending from South Dakota to southwestern Oklahoma. Of 138 specimens from the hybrid zone proper, all but three were hybrids. Further, within this zone orioles were common, indicating that the hybrids were fertile.

It was amply clear that, where they came together, these two orioles were hardly "reproductively isolated" and Sibley and Short proposed that they be considered a single species. This conclusion has been accepted by the great majority of American ornithologists. This is an example of how the status of a species can change when adequate material finally becomes available and is properly analyzed.

A recent study has shown that, in certain areas within the oriole hybrid zone studied in 1955-56, by 1974 the "Baltimore" and "Bullock's" types had largely "sorted out" and exist side by side with little hybridization (Corbin and Sibley, 1977). Apparently in these areas the hybrids do not survive as well as do the parental types. This change, which has occurred within the past 20 years, is a reminder that evolution is a continuing process and that natural situations are not static.

Thus far, the two examples that we have given deal with merging two species. A case of splitting involves the division of the Boat-tailed Grackle into two different species, a situation beautifully analyzed by Selander and Giller (1961). Two distinct subgroups can be recognized within these grackles, distinguished by differences in size, minor differences in plumage color, and differences in iris color. One group (yellow iris) occupies the coastal marshes of the southeastern United States; the other (brown iris) ranges from Texas, New Mexico, and Arizona south to northwestern South America. The differences between the two subgroups are so minor that ornithologists traditionally regarded them as belonging to a single species.

Selander and Giller documented important ecological and behavioral differences between the two groups. They also found a number of localities in extreme southeastern Texas and adjacent Louisiana in which pairs of both groups bred side by side, sometimes nesting in the same tree. Interestingly, on the basis of specimen and sight records, it appeared that the two groups were separate at one time but that the western group spread to the north and east starting about 1912 and eventually invaded the range of the eastern group. This conveniently set up the mixed breeding sites studied by Selander and Giller.

Despite the fact that the two groups breed in close proximity, no mixed mating was seen and no hybrid was ever found. Males of the western group attempted to mate with females of either group. It appeared that differences in the vocalizations and displays of the males of the two groups enabled the females to differentiate between them and select mates of their own group. Thus, despite the opportunity to form mixed pairs, the two populations remained reproductively isolated. Whereas "degree of difference" had led ornithologists down a false path, "reproductive isolation" indicated clearly that two distinct species were involved, an interpretation proposed by Selander and Giller and followed by the A.O.U. Check-list Committee.

If we merge, or "lump," two species such as the Baltimore and Bullock's orioles, each with its own name, the question arises: "Which name should we use for the new, enlarged species?"

If one looks at a field guide such as Peterson (1961) or Robbins et al (1966), one will find two names given for each species of bird. The first is in English and in Roman type, e.g., Brown Towhee; the second is usually derived from Latin or Greek, or at least latinized, and is in italic type, e.g., *Pipilo fuscus*. The first is the common, or vernacular, name, or perhaps more accurately in our case, the English name (Parkes, 1975). The second is the scientific name. The first word of the scientific name is always capitalized and refers to the genus, or group, to which the bird belongs. The second word is always lower case and refers to the particular species, or kind, of the bird.

In addition to the differences in the forms of these two names, there is another most important distinction. The English names are completely "unofficial" in that there are no widely recognized rules or regulations governing their makeup, and there is no body or agency charged with standardizing them. On the other hand, there is a most complex set of internationally recognized rules and regulations governing the makeup of the scientific names— The International Code of Zoological Nomenclature. In addition, an agency, the International Commission on Zoological Nomenclature, rules on how the code applies in individual cases if there is some dispute or uncertainty involved. Such a standardized international system of nomenclature is vital, as common names are not only unstandardized but the language in which they are written changes from country to country. But if the scientific name of an animal is used in an article or in a paper presented at a scientific meeting, scientists from England, India, or Brazil will know exactly what species of animal is being discussed.

When two species, each with its own scientific name, are merged, there is a definite rule in the International Code, the "Law of Priority," which governs which of the two names shall apply to the new, enlarged species. This law states that the older name—that is, the name given to the species first formally described as new—shall be the one used.

In the case of the orioles, we find that the Baltimore Oriole was first described in 1758 under the species name *"galbula"* by the Swedish zoologist Carl von Linné, better known to us as Linnaeus. The Bullock's Oriole was first described in 1827 under the species name *"bullockii"* by the English zoologist William Swainson. Under the Law of Priority the older species name, *galbula,* used for the Baltimore Oriole, prevails and the scientific name

Icterus galbula is used for the two merged species.

Regarding the English name, there is no official "law" to guide us. The A.O.U. Check-list Committee suggested "Northern Oriole" as an English name. In the case of the three former junco species now lumped into one, the name "Dark-eyed Junco" was suggested, and for the Audubon's and Myrtle warblers, the name "Yellow-rumped Warbler." A few years ago in a similar situation when the Red-eyed Towhee of the east and the Spotted Towhee of the west were lumped, the name "Rufous-sided Towhee" was suggested.

The tendency seems to be to select a third "neutral" name rather than the English name connected with the species first described. One may wonder if this is done, at least in part, so as not to miff either easterners or westerners. Usually there is an initial period in which everyone is miffed, but things eventually settle down. Although such English names are not at all official or binding, in time they are adopted by most persons and some degree of standardization is achieved.

Finally, we come to the question of what lumping two species does to one's life list. The birder who has seen both the Baltimore and Bullock's orioles suddenly finds that these two species are considered one by professional ornithologists. Does he or she eliminate these two species from the life list and substitute for them a single species, the Northern Oriole, thereby losing a species from the life list? Or, since the two former species are so readily distinguishable in the field, should the merger be ignored?

In an excellent discussion of birding, Small (1974) states that the life list "does not pretend any scientific merit and is kept for purely personal reasons." Nonetheless, it seems to us that if the life list is to have any real meaning, it should be based on current biological concepts and a system of nomenclature derived from them. To keep the Baltimore and Bullock's orioles on a life list because they can be easily identified in the field is to substitute the criterion of visual distinctness for the biological species concept. This simply goes back to the old idea of "degree of difference" as the major criterion for species recognition.

Further, it would be desirable to standardize life lists as much as possible rather than have each birder make arbitrary, individual decisions on what he or she wishes to include in, or eliminate from, the life list.

As may be realized from the examples of the Scrub Jay, professional ornithologists must sometimes make decisions regarding species status without having incontrovertible proof. The difficulty is compounded because we must fit a wide variety of natural situations into a rigid system of nomenclature. As a result, we find that there is a number of controversial cases in which there is some disagreement among ornithologists regarding species status. Fortunately, the number of such cases is small, and there is unanimous agreement on the great majority of North American bird species.

In the interests of biological reality and standardization, it seems wise to us to follow the conclusions reached by a permanent body concerned with making decisions in cases involving changes in the species status of North American birds. The only permanent body of this kind is the A.O.U. Check-list Committee. We grant that the conclusions of this committee are not binding, nor are they followed by all ornithologists, including the authors of this book. Nonetheless, the committee is made up of recognized authorities well versed in modern approaches to the species problem. We suggest, therefore, that life lists be based on the species included in whatever edition of the *Checklist of North American Birds* is current, as modified by the subsequent supplements published in *The Auk*. Since *American Birds* subscribes to this policy, birders can readily keep up with such changes as they are made. From this viewpoint, it is farewell to the Audubon's Warbler, the Bullock's Oriole, and the White-winged and Oregon juncos, among others.

3

THE BIRD YEAR

To THE EASTERN BIRDER, the year is sharply divided into seasons, and seasonal changes in the numbers and kinds of birds are pronounced. Especially dramatic is the change from winter to spring, with countless millions of birds of many species moving from southern wintering grounds to northern breeding grounds. These great waves of songbirds moving north through the east and midwest are eagerly anticipated by birders.

On the western seaboard, seasonality and seasonal changes in bird life are far less pronounced. In our milder, more even climate the proportion of resident species is greater and the proportion of migratory species smaller than in the more rigorous and more seasonally variable climates of the east and midwest. As a result, seasonal shifts in the numbers of species and individuals present are far less abrupt and dramatic. The changes in local avifaunas between winter and spring and between late summer and fall feature the gradual disappearance of a number of species and their gradual replacement by others. And this gentle transition from one season to another is superimposed on a relatively large number of resident species.

To illustrate the nature of seasonal change in the land birds of our area, we may consider the "bird year" at the Hastings Reservation. Although this area is somewhat removed from Monterey Bay, the kinds of land birds involved and the major events during the year are much the same as in the bay area proper. Further, the birds at Hastings have been kept under reasonably close observation for a number of years.

To begin with, the proportion of resident species at Hastings is relatively high. This may be seen by comparing the land birds found in the vicinity of New York City (Arbib et al., 1966) with the land birds found at the Hastings Reservation (Linsdale, 1947). We shall not consider aquatic, marsh, or shore birds, since these habitats are not represented at Hastings. Of the 179 species of land birds listed by Arbib et al. (1966) in their "Checklist and Calendar Graph," 33 species (18 percent) are resident; of 133 species at Hastings, 48 (36 percent) are resident. The possibilities for pronounced seasonal change are thus reduced in our area.

We may start our bird year at the Reservation early in September. Obviously, the year presented here is an "average" one. There is, of course, some annual variation in the exact timing of events, but what follows is typical of what happens in most years.

By early September, the summer visitants have left for the south, and the winter visitants have not yet arrived. The occasional "summer" bird that is seen is probably not a local bird but a late transient from farther north. For the birder, this is the dullest part of the year. Not only is the variety of species at its most limited, but the birds themselves are quiet and not much in evidence.

Between the middle and end of September, the first winter visitants arrive. A few Golden-crowns and White-crowns are seen or heard; some of the males, at least, sing occasionally. A few Red-breasted Sapsuckers, Hermit Thrushes, Ruby-crowned Kinglets, and Fox Sparrows move in. The latter part of September and the month of October see the arrival of additional winter species and a gradual buildup in the numbers of winter visitants. Flocks of "crown" sparrows increase in size, and junco flocks build up as more wintering birds from the Sierra Nevada and the north coast join the resident birds. The latter form the nucleus of the winter flocks (Sabine, 1959).

Some resident species shift their ranges somewhat in late October and early November as the weather becomes colder. Steller's Jays, Chestnut-backed Chickadees, and Purple Finches, restricted in summer to the higher parts of the Reservation or to cooler, more humid, and more heavily wooded canyon bottoms, expand their local distribution, with some individuals moving along stream drainages into more exposed, less wooded areas. The onset of the first appreciable rains and the subsequent appearance of new, green growth of annuals sees most of the California Quail moving from riparian and open grassland areas up into the blue-oak woodland. At this time, Golden-crowned Sparrows, the most "vegetarian" of our sparrows, with a diet almost 100 percent plant material (Martin et al., 1961), switch from a diet mainly of seeds to a diet mainly of green plants.

By the end of October the winter bird picture has been largely completed and the numbers of species and individuals are more or less stabilized. Occasional periods of stormy weather or a rare heavy snowfall may bring an influx of birds from higher elevations, but such changes are only temporary.

The first noticeable change in the winter picture actually involves no shifts in the numbers or kinds of birds, but is found in changes in the behavior of certain resident species. The first Rufous-sided Towhees start to sing between mid-January and early February. To the resident ornithologist, hearing these first brief, low-volume songs, the winter is over even though the wall calendar, low air temperatures, and snow-covered ridges in the distance say otherwise. For these songs are the first indication that the events leading to a new breeding season are under way. Also at this time Great Horned and Screech owls begin to call more often, and duets between male and female Great Horned Owls may be heard.

As time passes, a few juncos and Bewick's Wrens start to sing. The juncos are undoubtedly resident males; when resident and migrant subspecies of a given species winter together, the resident birds show breeding behavior and reach breeding condition earlier than do the migrants. By late February a few birds have started to nest. There are February nesting records at Hastings for the Anna's Hummingbird, Scrub Jay, and House Finch.

March is the "swing" month between the breeding and

nonbreeding seasons. More and more resident species start to
sing steadily and show territorial behavior, and chases and
combats become increasingly frequent. Even a few wintering
crown sparrows start to sing at this time.

March also marks the arrival of most of the summer visitant
species. These include the Turkey Vulture, Poor-will, Black-
chinned and Allen's hummingbirds, Western Flycatcher,
Violet-green Swallow, House Wren, Blue-gray Gnatcatcher,
Warbling Vireo, Orange-crowned and Black-throated Gray
warblers, and Northern Oriole. California Quail start to form
pairs within their coveys, and winter flocks of House Finches
break up into pairs. The level of song continues to rise.

The first half of April is the most enjoyable time of year for the
birder. Winter visitant species are still represented by at least a
few individuals and representatives of even the latest-arriving
summer visitant species have come in. These include the Western
Kingbird, Ash-throated Flycatcher, Western Wood Pewee,
Solitary Vireo, Yellow Warbler, Black-headed Grosbeak, Lazuli
Bunting, and Chipping Sparrow. Thus, the variety of species at
this time is the greatest of the year. In addition, singing is still at a
high level, and the trees are not yet fully leafed out, so that birds
are easy to locate. The pleasure of birding at this season is much
enhanced by fine weather and an abundance of wildflowers. In
the last half of April, nesting gets under way for a number of
resident species, although most pairs will wait until early May.

By early May the winter visitants have disappeared save for a
few individuals, probably late migrants moving up from the
south. Resident species such as the Steller's Jay, Chestnut-
Backed Chickadee, and Purple Finch, which extended their
ranges in winter, have once again retreated to their breeding
areas. Nesting is widespread. The period from late April to late
June accounts for by far the greater part of the nesting effort at
Hastings, and early May to mid-June is the heart of the nesting
season. Young of most species are much in evidence in late June,
joining the young from earlier nestings.

The latter half of July and August are marked by low activity. Birds are quiet and not much in evidence. Some of the summer-breeding species start to leave for the south by late July, and by the end of August the summer visitants have disappeared save for the occasional late migrant from the north. August and the first half of September are the poorest times of the year for the land birder, and the lack of variety and the hot weather make this the low point in the year. The situation does not improve until the winter visitants start to arrive about mid-September to start another "bird year."

To the birder, the different parts of the birding year mean good versus poor birding; lots of song and high activity versus periods of relative silence and low activity; times of great species variety versus periods of "resident birds only," and even these familiar species inactive and not doing much.

But the annual cycle involves much more than this. Vitally important events have occurred involving migration, reproduction, molt, and profound changes in behavior. All of these are worth examining in some detail. Further, it is obvious that the various events in the annual cycle occur in a definite sequence and according to a rather rigid schedule. Nothing is random or haphazard about this. We do not expect to see widespread nesting in January nor do we expect to hear widespread and steady singing at the height of the molt period. Obviously, these cyclical events are timed to occur in particular parts of the year. Let us examine, then, some of the factors that influence the annual cycle.

4

REPRODUCTION

THE MOST IMPORTANT single activity for any population of living organisms is reproduction, for without the production of future generations, no population can survive. And the survival of any species depends on the survival of at least one of the populations of which it is composed. Therefore, reproduction should occur under the conditions that are most favorable for its success.

Considering the year as a whole, even in the Monterey Bay area of relatively mild and even climate there is still considerable seasonal fluctuation in such environmental features as rainfall, sunshine, temperature, plant growth, insect abundance, and many others. Given such variation, it is evident that certain times of the year, or perhaps a particular time of the year, would be best for reproduction. At the same time reproduction, vital though it may be, is still only one of a number of critical activities and processes that must be carried out by any population of birds to insure its survival. Thus, reproduction, or any other highly important population activity or process, must be carried out at a time that is advantageous but at the same time would not disrupt other activities in the annual cycle.

With this background, we may ask: "What is the best time of year for reproduction in the birds of the Monterey Bay area?" To answer this question we must outline the events which are of critical importance to successful reproduction and see what demands they make on the environment.

The first step in the actual nesting cycle is the selection of a proper nest site, followed by construction of the nest. For most birds, adequate nest sites and building materials are in good supply over much of the year. Only species that have specialized nest requirements, such as hole nesters that depend on abandoned woodpecker holes, or birds that need mud or other special materials for nest construction, may find nest sites or building materials in short supply. In most years the birds of the Monterey Bay area are not limited by such shortages.

For birds locating the nest in deciduous trees or shrubs, however, it is advantageous to have at least some foliage developed to provide concealment for the nest. For such nesters, spring would be the season in which this advantage could be first realized.

Once the nest has been built, the next important step is the laying of a set, or "clutch," of fertile eggs. We shall defer discussion of pairing and mating to a later section, and focus here on egg production. For most of our land birds, four is very close to the number of eggs in a complete clutch. This means that a breeding female will have to manufacture a considerable amount of material, mainly protein, to accomplish normal laying. For example, the average weight of an egg laid by the subspecies of Brown Towhee resident in southern California is 4.29 g (Hanna, 1924), and a set of four would weigh about 17 g. The average weight of a breeding female of this subspecies is 41.5 g (Davis, 1951). A female laying an average set would thus have to manufacture an amount of material equivalent to 41 percent of her body weight. Similar demands on most Monterey Bay area songbirds for which information is available fall between 20 and 40 percent of body weight.

Since this "extra" material is composed mainly of proteins, there must be a source of such material readily available to breeding females if they are to lay successfully. Plant material is relatively low in proteins compared to animal matter. The most widespread and easily available source of animal proteins for a breeding female would be insects and closely related forms, such as spiders. Reproduction, then, should occur at a time of year when such food is abundant and easily obtained. In the Monterey Bay area, as in most North Temperate areas, insects are most abundant in the spring and summer months. From the standpoint of egg-laying, this part of the year would be the most favorable.

Regarding the eggs, they must be kept at a temperature high enough that normal development of the embryo will take place. This, of course, is accomplished by incubation by one parent, or by both in turn. Since the eggs must be left uncovered at times, as when an incubating parent leaves to forage, or leaves the nest as a predator approaches it, moderate or fairly high air temperatures are advantageous for successful development of the eggs. The spring and first half of the summer provide such conditions.

Next, we must consider the young after hatching. Most nestlings at hatching are poorly developed and have very little plumage. Therefore, they are very susceptible to both heat and cold in the early part of nest life. Even though they may be brooded by one of the parents or by both in turn, there are times, as with the eggs, when the young may be left unattended for long periods. Therefore moderate temperatures are also beneficial to the well-being of the young. In North Temperate areas such temperatures are found in the spring and early summer, after the chill of winter and before the extreme heat of late summer. Such timing is quite compatible with the timing of successful egg-laying and incubation.

Next we must know what kinds of food are necessary to raise the young to the point at which they can fend for themselves. Studies of nestling development indicate that their growth rate is extremely rapid. In the Willow (formerly Traill's) Flycatcher, for example, King (1955) found that the average weight of a nestling increased from 1.8 g on the first day of nest life to 13.3 g on the fourteenth day, when it left the nest. This is a weight increase of 739 percent in two weeks. Banks (1959) reported that the average weight of a Nuttall's White-crown nestling increased from 2.4 g on the first day to 19.0 g on the ninth, one day before leaving the nest, an increase of 792 percent.

Such weight increases result from the appearance of new structures and the further development of structures present at hatching. Nestlings demand a diet rich in proteins, since these are the building blocks from which these new materials are made. It is no coincidence, then, that the nestlings of nearly all songbirds are fed a diet of insects, spiders, and the like. And, as we have seen, insect abundance is at, or near, its peak in spring and summer.

Considering the demands made by egg-laying and successful raising of the young, it is not surprising that the greatest part of the breeding effort of the land birds of the Monterey Bay area occurs between April and July.

Thus far we have been discussing the reasons *why* a particular time of year would be best for reproduction, and *why* a particular breeding schedule has evolved in most Monterey Bay area birds. As biologists would put it, we have been discussing the "ultimate" factors in the timing of songbird breeding in the area. Granted that a particular period of time would be best for breeding, how can proper timing be achieved? Here we are thinking in terms of environmental variables such as cycles of daylength, of rainfall, of temperature, of sunshine, and others. These "proximate" factors serve to set in motion the physiological responses in the individual that lead to breeding and, in those species that have a self-starting, internal, physiological cycle, these proximate factors serve to keep such cycles properly timed. There is no aspect of scientific ornithology that has come in for more attention than the proximate factors involved in breeding, and the mechanisms are very intricate and difficult to understand in fine detail. But a general consideration of the subject makes a fascinating story.

To begin with, we must have some ideas of the structure and functioning of the reproductive organs, or gonads, of birds in order to understand avian reproductive cycles. Males have two testes, each of which has two important functions. Within each testis there are many much-convoluted tubules within which mature sperms are produced. Between the tubules there are aggregations of cells, the so-called *interstitial tissue*. Some of these cells are specialized to secrete male hormones (androgens), the effects of which we shall consider later. Thus, the testis serves both as a producer of sperms and as an endocrine gland. Both the tubules and the interstitial tissues undergo pronounced annual changes in structure and activity.

With the exception of some hawks and owls, female birds have only one ovary, the left; the right ovary has been reduced to a nonfunctional vestige. The ovary also has a dual function. It is the site of the production of mature *ova* (an *ovum* is that part of the egg that consists of a huge cell loaded with yolk) and it also functions as an endocrine gland, secreting a variety of hormones important to successful reproduction. The ovary contains a number of follicles, each of which contains a cell, the *oocyte,* which is potentially capable of developing into a mature ovum. Of the thousands of oocytes, only a few will reach maturity.

Associated with the ovary is the oviduct, a tube down which the mature ova pass after the follicles which contain them have ruptured. The mature ova are fertilized in the upper part of the oviduct and surrounded by albumin ("egg white") in the middle part. The shell membranes, shell, and shell pigments (if any) are added in the expanded lower part of the oviduct. The completed egg then moves to the vent and is extruded to the outside. Both the ovary and the oviduct also undergo pronounced annual cycles in size and activity.

Since the proximate factors in the male and female cycles are so different, we shall take them up separately. Most work has been done on the male cycle, and most of this research has been done on North Temperate birds.

Scientists became interested in the timing and control of avian breeding cycles many years ago. The early approach was to try to find some environmental phenomenon that has a pronounced annual cycle which, hopefully, would correlate with the cyclic nature of breeding. Most of the factors which were considered were climatic—annual cycles of rainfall, temperature, sunshine, humidity, and the like. Temperature was for many years thought to be the main controlling factor. However, at any specific locality such climatic factors show considerably more annual variation than does the timing of breeding cycles. Thus, the correlation between breeding time and climatic factors at any particular locality over a period of years was not very convincing.

It was not until the mid-1920s that any real advance was made. In the fall of 1924 William Rowan, a professor of zoology at the University of Alberta, Edmonton, Canada, started a simple but classic experiment that gave ornithologists the clue they had been seeking.

Rowan discarded the annual cycles of climatic factors as being too variable to account for the relative regularity of avian breeding and migration cycles in the North Temperate Zone. After considering a number of other factors, he concluded that the only widespread environmental phenomenon that was highly regular was the daylength, or *photoperiodic,* cycle. December 22 is the shortest day of the year at any North Temperate locality. After that date, daylength (sunrise to sunset) steadily increases until the longest day of the year is reached on June 21. Then the days shorten progressively until December 22. Not only is this cycle virtually unvarying at any particular locality, differing by only a few minutes a year, but birds have prominent sense organs, the eyes, that are indisputably sensitive to daylight.

In September 1924 Rowan captured a number of male Dark-eyed Juncos. This species breeds commonly at Edmonton and migrates somewhat farther south in fall. He divided the birds into a control group, caged in an outdoor aviary subjected to natural daylengths and temperatures, and an experimental group, caged in a similar aviary differing only in that it was provided with artificial light supplied by two ordinary 50-watt light bulbs. On October 1, he started to give the experimentals steadily increasing daylength by turning on the lights at sunset and leaving them on for five minutes longer each day than on the previous evening. By the end of December, when he autopsied the last experimental, the testes had increased in size so that they were larger than the testes of wild juncos arriving in Edmonton in spring. The testes of the controls were still at minimum winter size. Rowan published a brief paper on his results (Rowan, 1925), and in 1926 he repeated his experiments. By December 30, the gonads of the experimental males were larger than those of wild spring arrivals. As late as February 21, the gonads of the controls were still at minimum winter size (Rowan, 1926).

Rowan's publications started a veritable torrent of experimental work on this problem. For a while, it seemed as though everyone interested in avian breeding cycles was taking birds of one kind or another and subjecting them to lights of every color on all kinds of schedules. Much of this work was well done and served to corroborate Rowan's original findings. Some of it was on the crackpot side; one worker published a paper in a very respectable journal in which he claimed that he had exposed grain to long artificial days and that when he fed such grain to experimental male House Sparrows, they came into breeding condition. When other workers tried to confirm this, predictably they came up with negative results.

In the decades since Rowan did his pioneering work, many advances have been made in working out the mechanisms involved in timing the avian testis cycle. The problem has been complicated by the fact that not all species which have been studied have shown the same pattern of response. Nonetheless, for most Temperate Zone male birds, increasing amounts of light enter the brain via the eyes and perhaps in part directly through the skull as days lengthen in late winter and early spring. The increasing amounts of light trigger a very complicated mechanism in the brain, involving the hypothalamus and the anterior pituitary; the details are beyond the scope of this discussion. It is this mechanism, set in motion by increasing daylength, that brings the male into full reproductive condition in the spring, some weeks ahead of the female.

The males of some species seem to have internal breeding rhythms, the fine timing of which is accomplished by the photoperiodic cycle. In either case, photoperiod is of critical importance in keeping the cycle regular and on time.

The changes that the testes undergo from the resting state, when they are small and inactive, to breeding condition are pronounced. They begin to increase in size as the tubules within them increase in length and diameter. At the same time, resting cells within the tubules begin a long and complicated series of divisions and transformations which eventually results in the production of mature sperms. The increase in testis size is enormous. In the Nuttall's White-crown at Berkeley, a single testis enlarged from a volume of 0.5 mm^3 to a volume of 140 mm^3, an increase of 280 times (Blanchard, 1941). In the Dark-eyed Junco, the testes of males resident in Berkeley increased from a volume of 0.5 mm^3 to a maximum of 200 mm^3 (Wolfson, 1942).

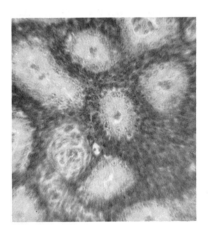 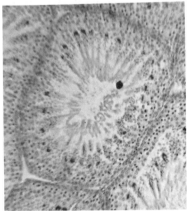

Photomicrographs of testes of male House Sparrows collected on September 18 *(left)* and on May 24 *(right)*. The September testis (non-breeding) is small (greatest diameter 1 mm) and inactive, with small tubules lined with a single row of resting cells. The May testis (breeding) has a greatest diameter of 10 mm, and the tubules are much enlarged. Bundles of mature sperms, darkly stained, are nearest the center of each tubule. Magnification 1000×. (R. Buchsbaum)

In both species these changes occurred between mid-December and the end of March. Changes of similar magnitude and rate have been reported in a number of species.

At the same time, the hormone-secreting cells of the interstitial tissue increase in numbers and secretory activity. The increased level of male hormones that results has a profound effect on male behavior and is responsible for the behavioral changes associated with males in the early part of the breeding cycle.

The factors that bring the male cycle to an end are not known. In most North Temperate species it ends shortly after the breeding season, and the male then enters a *refractory period*. The testes rapidly decrease in size and the tubules become cleared of the cellular debris resulting from the period of intense gonadal activity. In this refractory period, the testes will not respond to light no matter how massive the dose. It is not known definitely whether it is the testes or the brain that fails to respond. At any rate, this is a period of gonadal rest and reorganization following the breeding season. After some weeks in this refractory state, the male will again respond to stimulation by light.

The length of the refractory period varies from species to species. Following this period, the males of some species show a mild response to the still long days of early fall. However, because the days are becoming shorter, the response is moderate at best and it is ended by the short days of late fall, the testes again becoming inactive. In some species there is no autumnal response at all.

The female cycle is markedly different from that of the male. Although ovarian growth and development can be triggered by increased photoperiod in many species, light alone cannot bring the oocytes to much more than halfway development. The female appears to depend on psychological stimuli such as the courtship behavior of the male and on the visual stimuli provided by certain environmental features such as increase in insect abundance, to bring her into full breeding condition. The exact physiological mechanisms involved are not known at present.

Like the testes, the ovary shows a pronounced seasonal cycle of size and activity. Unlike the testes, which develop more or less steadily once they have started their active phase, the ovary undergoes a lengthy period of barely perceptible growth and change and then, in a short period just before the nesting season, develops very rapidly to full size and activity. For example, in the Starling in Connecticut the ovary showed a very low rate of growth over a period of 108 days and then grew and developed to laying condition in 26 days (Bissonnette and Zujko, 1936). The female reaches breeding condition some time after the male.

In response to estrogen and other hormones produced by the developing ovary, the oviduct grows rapidly and becomes much convoluted. By the time of laying, the duct is ready to receive mature ova and complete the process of egg formation. The female cycle ends shortly after the laying of the last clutch of eggs. Partly developed follicles are resorbed and the ovary and oviduct rapidly decrease in size. What ends the cycle is not known.

In addition to the changes in the gonads associated with breeding, most (but not all) species of birds also develop a bare area on the abdomen shortly before incubation. This is the so-called *incubation patch* (or *brood patch*), and it develops under the influence of certain hormones. Some of the abdominal down feathers drop and the skin thus left bare becomes much thickened and invaded by blood vessels. This will be discussed further under **Nesting.**

As may be seen, the timing of reproduction in Monterey Bay area birds results from a very complicated and finely tuned mechanism which functions so that breeding occurs at the most favorable time of year. This is undoubtedly why the females are not tied to photoperiod as rigidly as are the males and why they reach full breeding condition only in response to favorable environmental conditions. If the females were timed as precisely as the males, there would be too much inflexibility in the whole system, and no adjustment could be made if favorable nesting conditions should be delayed or absent in a given year. When favorable conditions are absent, the females of a population may simply fail to reach full breeding condition, and no energy is wasted on a futile reproductive effort. It is also advantageous for the males to reach breeding condition ahead of the females, as the male must carry out certain critical activities before nesting starts. This will be discussed later.

Finally, one may ask, what of birds that live on or near the Equator, where daylength is constant or nearly so? In many equatorial populations one may find some breeding in most, or all, months of the year. However, there are definite peaks of breeding even in most equatorial populations. These appear to be timed by factors such as the annual cycles of rainfall (Miller, 1962), of sunshine and ambient temperature (Davis, 1971), and others.

5

BREEDING BEHAVIOR

BY BREEDING BEHAVIOR we mean not just copulation, nesting, and the raising of young to independence but also song, territoriality, courtship, and pair formation as well. These events, involving both males and females, are controlled by a complicated series of hormones which insure that the different parts of the entire breeding program occur in the right sequence and at the proper times. Since song is important in several aspects of breeding behavior and is often the first indication that a bird is starting its breeding cycle, we shall consider it first.

Song

There is abundant evidence from the laboratory that hormones have profound effects on the singing of male birds. Injection of testosterone into males of a number of species has caused them to sing at times of the year well removed from the breeding season. There is also indirect evidence from field studies that hormones are important in this regard. In the Rufous-sided Towhee, song is first heard at the time that the cells in the testes which produce steroid sex hormones begin to multiply, and song spreads in the population as the testes become increasingly active (Davis, 1958).

Before considering song as such, we must give the reader one warning. The observer of animal behavior must be constantly on guard to avoid *anthropomorphism,* the interpretation of nonhuman phenomena in terms of human emotions and experience. And nowhere is there such a strong tendency to be anthropomorphic as in the interpretation of bird song. Because humans often sing when they are happy and because many bird songs are pleasing or beautiful to the human ear, they have been equated with everything from shouts of exultation to religious music. One has only to read Dawson's (1923) account of the Hermit Thrush to see how far off the deep end one can plunge in this regard.

Bird song has two functions. First, a male defending a territory sings to warn other males of his species that a particular area is already occupied by a conspecific (belonging to the same species) male ready to defend it. In this context, song is a hostile vocalization that means KEEP OUT! Warning song is most advantageous as it keeps most conspecific males away from the singer's territory, thus avoiding direct confrontations and fights which use up time and energy and may lead to injury. Even when a strange male does trespass, an approach by the defender, accompanied by rapid, intense singing, is often enough to make the intruder flee.

Second, song announces the presence of the singing male to unmated females of his own species, since such females recognize the song as coming from a conspecific male. Thus, the singer attracts a potential mate. And it may be noted that the buzzy, unmusical (to the human ear) song of the Black-throated Gray Warbler serves just as efficiently in mate attraction as does the ethereal (also to the human ear) song of the Hermit Thrush.

An avian vocalization may be properly classified as song only if it serves one or both of these functions. A few birds, such as the Brown Towhee, have two different songs, one used for territorial advertising, the other for mate attraction. We can tell that one of these songs is used only for mate attraction as it is given only by unmated males and is no longer given after the singer has attracted a mate and a pair has been formed (Quaintance, 1938).

In some species, sound production other than singing serves to advertise territory and attract a mate. The drumming of woodpeckers (done with the bill against a resistant surface) and of the Ruffed Grouse (done by the wings beating against air) is not truly song, as these sounds are not produced vocally, but it is the functional equivalent of song.

The amount of singing done by a male of a given species may vary a great deal seasonally, depending on what stage of the breeding cycle he has reached. The unmated male Western Flycatcher, when he arrives early in spring, sings a great deal from dawn to dusk when he is establishing a territory; after a pair has been formed, song is given only briefly just before dawn to advertise territory, and the male sings no more during the rest of the day (Davis et al., 1963). In the Song Sparrow, the amount of singing varies with the stage of the nesting cycle (Nice, 1943). In the Rufous-sided Towhee there is a noticeable drop-off in singing in the first half of April, after which song output returns to its previous level and remains high until the end of June (Davis, 1958). In general, unmated males are more persistent singers than are mated birds.

As we noted earlier, a few males of some species may show a mild gonadal response to the still-long days of fall following the refractory period. Such males may sing occasionally, but as the days continue to shorten the response wanes and singing is no longer heard.

Ornithologists have long been interested in how much of a given species' song is inherited and how much is learned by hearing other conspecific males sing. A number of cases have been investigated, and there is a great deal of interspecific variation. In some species nearly all song characteristics are inherited; in others nearly all are learned; and some fall between these extremes.

An especially well investigated case concerns the Nuttall's White-crown. Marler and Tamura (1964) took a number of nestlings, some only three days old, into the laboratory. Some were raised in isolation, others in groups of three or four, in soundproof chambers. When these birds reached maturity the following spring, they sang "naive" songs quite unlike the White-crown song, and there was considerable individual variation among them. However, their songs did contain certain elements which are characteristic of songs of the genus *Zonotrichia,* which includes the White-crown and several other species. These *"Zonotrichia"* elements had apparently been inherited and not learned.

Birds banded as nestlings and brought into the laboratory when 30 to 100 days old and isolated in soundproof chambers sang typical White-crown songs at maturity. Birds exposed to tape-recorded White-crown songs between the ages of three and 14 days sang "naive" songs at maturity, but birds exposed to such songs when 20 days old or older sang typical White-crown songs the following spring. This means that nestlings of this species must reach a certain stage of maturity and/or be exposed to a certain minimum amount of the singing of the male parent and other males within earshot before they learn the proper song. Taped songs of the Song Sparrow and the Harris' Sparrow (another member of the genus *Zonotrichia*) had no effect on the subsequent singing of nestling White-crowns of any age, indicating that these young birds had an inherited predisposition to learn the song of their own species. After further study Marler (1970) concluded that the critical period of song development in the young White-crown is from one week after hatching to two months old.

There is a question as to what is more important in song learning, the syllables (notes) themselves, or the overall song pattern, that is, the arrangements of the syllables in a song. This question has recently been investigated by Marler and Peters (1977) using young of the Swamp Sparrow, a close relative of the Song Sparrow and occurring in the same kind of habitat as that species. Using normal songs of Swamp and Song sparrows recorded in the field, these investigators made up a number of synthetic tapes, presenting various combinations of Swamp and Song sparrow characteristics. Swamp Sparrow syllables were arranged in Song Sparrow patterns, and Song Sparrow syllables in Swamp Sparrow patterns. When these tapes were played to young Swamp Sparrows reared in soundproof chambers, the experimental birds invariably selected Swamp Sparrow syllables in the songs they learned, indicating that the syllables themselves, and not the overall song pattern, are critical in song learning.

Another important question involves individual recognition of song. It is known from playing back tape-recorded songs and observing the listener's reaction that a bird of a given species will recognize and react to the song of his own species. But can the individual recognize the singing of a particular individual of its own species?

Marler and Isaac (1960) studied variation in the singing of male Brown Towhees in Mexico. Individual variation in some parts of the songs they taped was low, in other parts quite high. They hypothesized that the "standard" parts of the song served for species recognition and that the individually variable parts of the song served to identify a particular bird. In unmated male Brown Towhees of our area, the song consists of two parts. The first is an accelerating series of clear, metallic *chink* notes which varies little from one singer to another. A human observer hearing this at once identifies the bird as a Brown Towhee. The second part consists of two or three terminal notes which vary greatly from one singer to another. These could serve very well to identify a particular male to conspecifics nearby.

Falls (1969) and his colleagues played tape-recorded White-throated Sparrow songs to males of that species which were settled on territories. The reaction of a male to the song of a strange bird, recorded in an area out of earshot, was far stronger than his reaction to the singing of a neighbor. Such field experiments provide good evidence that a bird can recognize not only the singing of its own species, but the singing of particular individuals of its own species as well.

Territory

When we speak of birds' territories, we refer primarily to areas which are occupied in the breeding season. There have been many definitions of territory. Perhaps the best is that of Pitelka (1959), who defines it as "an exclusive area." This means simply that the owner of a territory is the only member of his species, except his mate and young, that uses it. This situation usually comes about in two ways. First, the owner may actively *defend* his exclusive area against trespassers of his own species. Second, birds of his own species may *avoid* any area that is already occupied by a conspecific. A true territory should not be confused with the "individual distance" which a bird in a flock maintains between itself and the bird nearest it.

As with any aspect of bird biology, we find great interspecific variation in bird territories. They are usually defended only in the breeding season, but some species (for example, Wrentit, California Thrasher, Brown Towhee) defend the same territory year-round. Others, such as the Mockingbird, defend only a portion of the breeding territory in winter, reoccupying the larger area in the breeding season (Michener and Michener, 1935). In most species of hummingbirds, the male defends one territory, the female another. The female comes to the male's territory for copulation, then nests in her own territory, raising the young by herself. Social birds such as the Acorn Woodpecker have a group territory defended jointly by the members of the group (MacRoberts and MacRoberts, 1976).

Although territories are usually defended only, or almost entirely, against conspecifics, some species may also drive out other kinds of birds as well. The Song Sparrow expels most other species as well as its own (Nice, 1943), and a male Western Flycatcher drove out some, but not all, trespassers of 14 other species (Davis et al., 1963). Acorn Woodpeckers chase other birds, and small mammals as well, from their group territories (MacRoberts and MacRoberts, 1976).

There are many types of territories, but two are especially common in the birds of our area. Most of them maintain a rather large territory in the breeding season. Within this area, courtship, pair formation, copulation, nesting, and feeding of both the parents and the young take place. This is the "classic" territory found in most birds. The second type is characteristic of colonial birds and is far smaller. Mating and nesting, or nesting only, take place within its boundaries, and feeding is carried out elsewhere in a communal foraging area. For example, the Brandt's Cormorant defends an area just large enough to support courtship, pair formation, copulation, and nesting (Williams, 1942). The Cliff Swallow defends only the nest itself (Emlen, 1952). The presence of large foraging grounds nearby, which one pair of birds could not possibly defend successfully, allows many territories to be packed into a relatively small area. In the case of

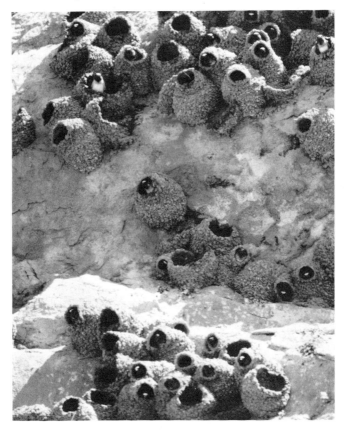

Cliff Swallow nests, showing the characteristic retort shape. (F. Lanting)

the cormorants, the foraging area is the ocean adjacent to the nesting colony; in the swallows it is the air space above it.

In resident species which form winter flocks, such as the Dark-eyed Junco, the birds form a dominance hierarchy, or peck order. In late winter, males begin to show increased intolerance of other members of the flock. This results in expansion "of the narrow spacing tolerated in the . . . winter flock into the wider spacing characteristic of the breeding season" (Sabine, 1955). The dominant male in the winter peck order and his mate retain the flock area as their breeding territory, and the other birds disperse to other areas. Much the same thing happens in winter flocks of the Carolina Chickadee in Texas, with the dominant pair using part of the winter flock range as a breeding territory (Dixon, 1963).

Birds such as the Wrentit and Brown Towhee, which mate for life and defend the same territory throughout the year, may be remarkably sedentary. A Wrentit banded at the Hastings Reservation was trapped a total of 13 times between February 9, 1942, and January 27, 1954. All trap records were confined to an area of 1.3 acres. Erickson (1938) found that Wrentit territories ranged from 0.5 to 2.75 acres, averaging 0.8 acre. Although this bird's retrap record was very spotty, the data suggest strongly that it lived within the same small territory for virtually 12 years. Even species such as this become more tolerant of intruders in the winter, and a pair may allow a strange conspecific to forage in their territory. In late winter such strangers are driven out as the pair reasserts ownership before the breeding season (Erickson, 1938). Davis (1957) noted trios of foraging Brown Towhees many times from August through February, but only pairs or single birds from March through June.

In migratory species the males usually arrive on the breeding grounds somewhat ahead of the females. They at once start to prospect for territories and lay claim to them. Very quickly the males start to settle in the areas which they will use for breeding; singing is intense as they advertise their claims. Territorial boundaries are adjusted by a series of contacts with neighbors, and combats among neighboring males are not uncommon at this time. In the Northern (or Red-necked) Phalarope the female selects and defends the territory, and the females arrive on the breeding grounds first (Tinbergen, 1935).

In addition to song, many species have "threat displays" which serve to intimidate intruders. A migrant Song Sparrow returning to his previous year's territory and finding a stranger there "goes into a specialized threat-display. . . . He *puffs himself out* into the shape of a ball; . . . he *holds one or both wings upright and vibrates them;* and he *sings softly. . . .*" (Nice, 1943). Specialized displays of this kind are found in many species. When an owner actually drives a trespasser from his territory, he may give a specialized "threat note." Mockingbirds give a "growl" or make a "growl-like noise" (Michener and Michener, 1935), Brown Towhees give "snarling, throaty notes" (Davis, 1957), and Western Flycatchers give a series of harsh *chrrip* notes when chasing intruders out of their territories (Davis et al., 1963). The importance of territory is indicated by the evolution of such specialized threat displays and vocalizations which make territorial defense more effective.

A bird near the center of his territory is invincible in combats with other conspecifics. The farther he gets from the center, the less successful he will be. In most cases territorial boundaries are not comparable to a rigid structure like a fence but should be thought of as a zone within which the outcomes of confrontations among owners of adjacent territories are variable. If the winner of such a "border" skirmish ventures farther into the strange territory, he is at the same time moving farther from the center of his own, and at a certain point he will retreat when confronted.

What are the advantages of the typical, multipurpose territory? First, it provides a site that ensures the orderly sequence of events in the breeding cycle. Nest site, nest materials, and an adequate food supply for parents and young are all at hand when needed. Second, territorial behavior serves to strengthen the attachment

between the members of the pair (the *pair bond*). Third,
territoriality reduces the chances of individuals remaining
unmated by distributing birds regularly throughout the habitat,
thereby making it easier for potential mates to find one another.
Finally, territoriality may reduce predation on a breeding
population by dispersing the members of the population and
locating them in areas with which they are intimately familiar.

In most breeding populations a number of birds fail to obtain a
territory or a mate. Such birds are called "floaters," and they
serve the important function of providing replacements for birds
which die or desert their mates. Such "floaters" are apparently on
the lookout for a vacancy, as one will move very quickly into a
territory which has lost a member of the resident pair.

Courtship and Pair Formation

After a male has established a territory, the next step in the
breeding sequence is the attraction of a female and the formation
of a pair. As we have noted, the singing of the male is of primary
importance in announcing his whereabouts to a prospective
mate. In migratory birds, with the males arriving first, most
territorial boundaries have been established by the time the
females arrive. Resident males which do not remain paired
throughout the year must again go through the process of finding
a mate. Those males of resident species which pair for life, such as
the Wrentit and Brown Towhee, whose mates have died must
advertise for a new partner. And males breeding for the first
time, regardless of species, must settle on a territory and attract a
mate if they can.

All of these cases involve a "landed" male trying to attract a
female and form a pair which will last at least through the
breeding season. The unmated female, on the other hand, seeks a
male with a suitable territory. A "landless" male will not attract a
mate, and a male with an inadequate territory has little chance
of doing so.

The actual formation of a pair is rarely seen in those species which hold a relatively large territory, as the observer must be on the spot at the exact moment a female first enters the male's territory if he is to observe the entire sequence of events which follows. Pair formation is more likely to be seen in colonial birds in which many males, each holding a small territory, are trying to attract females.

Williams (1942) has given a detailed description of the formal ceremonies leading to pair formation in Brandt's Cormorant, which nests in closely packed colonies in rocky situations where the birds are easily seen. Although the sexes are similar in appearance and voice, females have no difficulty recognizing males because of the elaborate displays given by the latter. The sex of females visiting the displaying males is apparently recognized by the latter. Perhaps this is because of the females' posture; Williams describes them as moving about "with thin, outstretched necks, peering at one advertiser and then another and exhibiting a tentative air as they move hesitantly among . . . the males."

In noncolonial birds in which the sexes differ in appearance and/or voice, there may also be characteristic displays given by territorial males to visiting females. For example, when a female Black-headed Grosbeak enters a male's territory, the male makes a series of nuptial flights, flying up and away from his perch and circling with wings outstretched and tail spread, singing all the while (Weston, 1947). In the Snow Bunting the first reaction of a male to an approaching female is to assume a threat posture, even though the sexes are easily distinguishable. If the female lands in his territory, the male at once spreads his wings and tail, turns his back to the female to display the striking black-and-white parts of his plumage, and then runs from her. He returns and repeats this performance a number of times (Tinbergen, 1939).

Nice (1943) described a somewhat intermediate situation in the Song Sparrow. The sexes are similar in appearance, but the female has certain distinctive vocalizations which identify her sex to a territorial male. His response to a female entering his territory is to swoop down suddenly over her, sometimes colliding with her, sometimes barely missing her, giving a loud song as he flies away. This performance is repeated a number of times. Nice called this display "pouncing."

A still different situation is found in species in which the sexes look and sound alike. Sargent (1940) described the formation of a pair of California Thrashers; the male had been color-banded, and the female consistently carried her wings in a drooping manner, allowing the observer to identify her as the same individual. The male lost his mate on December 9. On January 4 the new female appeared, and the male chased her from his territory. She was seen many times in his territory after this, always being chased by him. By January 21 the chasing had become less frequent and less vigorous. Between February 5 and March 6 she was tolerated and no chase was seen. There were several brief chases on March 6 and one, the final one, on March 10. The two started nest-building on the 12th and behaved as a mated pair until observations ceased on June 1.

Dilger (1956) made a most careful study in New York of pair formation in several species of thrushes in which the sexes look and sound alike. All are migratory, arriving on the breeding grounds in late April or May, in contrast to the California Thrasher, which is permanently resident. Therefore, the thrushes have a much more limited time for breeding, and pair formation must be rapid. The following account applies to all the species studied by Dilger.

When a strange conspecific of either sex enters a male's territory, it is at once chased by the owner. An intruding male promptly leaves the territory; an intruding female flees from the owner but stays inside the territorial limits. Chases become somewhat circular as the male continues to pursue the female. Frequently both male and female give threat displays. After a day or two, the frequency and intensity of chasing decreases, and after three or four days the male accepts the female and a pair has been formed.

In many species there is mutual hostility in the early stages of pair formation and this sometimes persists long after the pair has been formed. For example, in the Western Flycatcher both male and female frequently gave the *chrrip* threat note when they came together near the nest when feeding young, and in one pair actual chases were frequently seen when the female left the nest after a period of incubation or brooding. Early in the nesting cycle the male chased the female most of the time; then came an intermediate period in which each member of the pair chased the other about the same number of times; then came a final period in which the female chased the male far more frequently than he chased her (Davis et al., 1963). Similar shifts in dominance, from male to female, have been described in the Chaffinch (Marler, 1956) and other species. The important point is that relations between the members of a pair may include marked hostility but not enough to prevent successful breeding.

In some species the female nests in an area different than that occupied by the male and comes to his territory solely to copulate. We noted previously that this is the case in hummingbirds. Perhaps the most interesting of such cases involves species in which the males perform *lek* displays. A lek, or display ground, consists of an area, often used from year to year, in which a number of males gather, each holding a small territory, or "court," sometimes only a few feet square. Females come to the lek, and whenever a female appears, the males present at once start to give high-intensity courtship displays. The female moves about among the displaying males, finally selecting one as her mate. Copulation ensues and the female then retreats to her own nesting area, the males having nothing to do with care of eggs or young. The males spend only part of the day on the lek, and forage, rest, and roost elsewhere. The Sage Grouse, whose range extends into California east of the Sierra Nevada-Cascade axis, is a well-known lek species.

The lek situation differs from that described for the Brandt's Cormorant in that, in the latter, nesting also occurs in the male's territory. In the case of hummingbirds and lek birds, the male is promiscuous, mating with any female that will accept him. In these birds, courtship produces not a pair, but a fertilized female.

Some species are at least partly *polygamous,* some males or females having more than one mate. *Polygyny,* in which a male has more than one mate, has been reported in many species. It is not uncommon in some North Temperate wrens. Williams (1952) found a fair amount of polygyny in the Brewer's Blackbird; some marked males which he followed for two or more years were *monogamous* (single-mated) one year, polygynous the next.

A most unusual case of probable polygyny was reported in the Parula Warbler nesting in Point Lobos State Reserve by Williams et al (1958). This eastern and midwestern species had never been recorded in California until two females and one or two males appeared at Point Lobos in the spring of 1952. One of the males, if indeed there were originally two, later disappeared. Both females nested and must have been fertilized by the same male. He divided his time at first between the two nests but eventually settled at one. The unusual circumstance of an isolated breeding population of one male and two females apparently led to polygyny in a species in which such behavior had never been reported.

Polyandry, a female's having more than one mate, is rare in birds.

Promiscuity refers to cases "in which a member of one sex copulates with more than one member of the other but no lasting bond is formed" (Verner and Willson, 1966).

In some species the young remain with their parents, forming family groups which may last for several years. In such species, many yearlings (hatched the previous season) and some two-year olds assist the parents, sharing with them the duties of incubation, brooding, feeding the young, and protecting the nest from predators. Such "helpers at the nest" have been reported in about 80 species (Fry, 1972), including the Florida population of the Scrub Jay (Woolfenden, 1975), and the Acorn Woodpecker (MacRoberts and MacRoberts, 1976).

6

NESTING

BY NESTING we mean the sequence of events which starts
with the selection of the nest site and ends with the achieving of
independence by young out of the nest. Between these end points
we have nest construction, laying, incubation, hatching, care of
the nestlings, departure of fledglings from the nest, and care of
dependent young out of the nest. There is such great interspecific
variation in all aspects of nesting that we shall present the subject
in general terms only.

Those interested in detailed information should consult Alexander Skutch's
recently published monograph, *Parent Birds and Their Young* (1976), which
presents a wealth of interesting information on nesting, written in a very
readable and easily understood manner. Kendeigh (1952) also presents a great
deal of well-organized information on this subject.

Selection of the Nest Site

By nest site we mean the exact spot in which the nest is built. In
a species such as the Brandt's Cormorant, the nest fills most of the
male's territory and it is obvious that he has selected the nest site.
However, information on site selection is hard to come by in
species that hold relatively large territories, and one must spend
much time trying to follow both members of the pair to determine
which one makes the choice.

Really convincing information is lacking for most land birds.
Data such as those presented by Lawrence (1967) for four species
of woodpeckers, and by Nice (1943) for the Song Sparrow are
exceptional. In these species either male or female selects the nest
site, although in three species of woodpeckers the male made the
choice most of the time. In the Long-billed Marsh Wren the male

selects the nest site and builds most of the nest (Verner, 1965). In species such as the Phainopepla, in which the male builds all, or nearly all, of the nest and sometimes chases the female from the partly completed structure, it is likely that he also chooses the site. And in species such as hummingbirds and "lek" birds, the female obviously makes the choice. But good, clearcut information is lacking for nearly all of our passerines.

Nest Construction

The location, form, size, and composition of nests also vary greatly. An Anna's Hummingbird nest described by Kelly (1955) had outside measurements of 4.5 cm across the top by 4 cm deep. At the other extreme are nests of the Osprey, some of which may be used each year for decades by a succession of breeding pairs. Since new material is added each year, the nests grow larger and larger, and Bent (1937) described an old nest that had reached a height of 3 meters when the supporting tree collapsed. Nor does the size of the nest depend on the size of the builder. The Common Nighthawk, which weighs about 70 g, usually lays eggs on the bare ground, bare rock, or the flat, graveled roofs of city buildings; no nest is built. The Bushtit, which weighs about 5.5 g, builds an elaborate, pouchlike, hanging nest that averages 24 cm long (Addicott, 1938).

In some groups of birds there are definite similarities among species. Woodpeckers nest in holes that they excavate in trees. Vireos build beautifully fashioned, cuplike nests suspended from a twig or, more often, from a forked branchlet. But in the Family Paridae (titmice, chickadees, and others), the Bushtit builds the elaborate nest described above; the Plain Titmouse places its nest in tree cavities; and the Verdin of our deserts builds a ball-like nest usually located in a thorny shrub. The nest location may differ even between closely related species. The Brown Towhee nests in low bushes or small trees but the Rufous-sided Towhee is predominantly a ground-nester.

Cohen (1899) made the interesting observation that Rufous-sided Towhees that he observed shifted from ground-nesting to tree-nesting when the area became infested with feral house cats but began to nest on the ground again after he rid the area of these predators. The Common Yellowthroat, which places its nest no more than a few feet above ground or water in marsh vegetation, shows a similar ability to adapt to altered circumstances. When its nesting grounds in tule marshes at the northern ed of Clear Lake, Lake County, were under water because of floods, many nests were placed in trees, as high as 23 feet above ground (Johnson, 1904). These observations suggest that a species may modify its nesting habits in response to local changes.

In some species the male builds the nest, in some the female, in some both. The male may bring the nest material to the female, who does the actual construction; in other species the operation is just reversed. The time spent in nest-building also varies greatly. The Mourning Dove takes one to six days to build a nest; most nests take two or three days to complete (Cowan, 1952). Compare this to the Yellow-billed Magpie that builds each year a bulky domed, or roofed, nest composed of sticks, mud, and a nest bowl lined with grass and fine rootlets. Both members of the pair build, and nest construction occupies between four and eight weeks (Linsdale, 1937, Verback, 1973).

Nest materials also vary greatly, and it is useless to try to categorize them. The amount of material put into a nest is sometimes surprising. Verbeek (1973) dismantled a nest of the Yellow-billed Magpie. It contained 1,573 sticks and was plastered together with mud and cow dung. The total weight, including the lining, was a little over 11 kg. As Verbeek noted, this is about 70 times the weight of an adult magpie. Since the average Yellow-billed Magpie goes through seven or eight breeding seasons and pairs for life, a pair would gather, transport, and utilize between 80 and 90 kg of nest material in the course of a lifetime.

Birds holding territories large enough to supply breeding needs find nest materials within their territories unless some special material such as mud is needed. In such cases the builder(s) may have to obtain critical material from a source that is shared with other birds. Nest builders tend to be opportunistic, and when breeding near human habitation may use many unnatural materials. Western Flycatcher nests near houses and barns contained thread, string, burlap, paper, dust kittens, human hair, yarn, horsehair, straw, wood chips, and onion skin. One nest was fashioned mainly from dog hair which the builder had gathered from a nearby hedge against which dogs had scratched, leaving tufts of hair (Davis et al., 1963).

In some colonial species the shape of the nest may be important. Emlen (1952) studied the breeding of a colony of Cliff Swallows. This strongly colonial species packs many mud nests into a small space; the nest is the territory. It is retort shaped, with a curved entrance tunnel leading into the globular nest chamber. The tunnel entrance is defended vigorously. When nests are built side by side, sharing a common wall, the entrance tunnels are built so that they curve away from each other. Thus direct contact, and accompanying fights, are avoided by close neighbors as they come and go. When two nests are built opposite each other, fights are common between builders until the curved entrance tunnels are completed. Again, they curve away from each other, and the level of fighting drops sharply.

As we have seen, there is great interspecific variation in location, size, form, materials, and mode of construction among nests. There is one feature common to all, however—they work.

Laying and Clutch Size

Despite the great interspecific variation in all aspects of nesting discussed thus far, we may state unequivocally that in every known species of bird, the eggs are laid by the female. All females of a given species are either *determinate* or *indeterminate* layers. The former deposit the normal number of eggs and then cease laying even if one or more eggs have been lost or destroyed while the clutch was being completed; the "short" set is incubated. An indeterminate layer will stop producing eggs only when the clutch has reached proper size; any egg(s) lost before that point will be replaced. Phillips (1887) removed an egg a day from the nest of a Common Flicker, always leaving one egg in the nest. This female laid 71 eggs in 73 days! Such experiments have been carried out for a number of species in the field and in the aviary. The available data suggest that the females of most species are determinate layers, although much more information is needed to support any firm generalization.

If a nest is destroyed anytime after construction has started and before the young leave, the female may start a new nest. This depends in part on how late in the season the loss occurs and in part on the individual female. Some may attempt three or four nestings in a season and others may quit after the loss of the first nest.

In some species, eggs are laid one a day until the clutch is complete, but many are irregular, skipping one or more days during the laying period. There may also be intraspecific (within a single species) variation in this regard. At 12 nests of the Western Flycatcher, laying was regular in three and irregular in nine (Davis et al., 1963); whether the nest was early or late in the season did not matter. Laying can be rather arduous. Betty Davis watched a female Western Flycatcher deposit an egg; the process took five minutes and involved considerable hard straining.

The size of the "normal" clutch shows great interspecific variation. We have noted previously that four is close to the average clutch size for most small or medium-size Temperate Zone passerines, but there can be marked variation even within a given species. For example, average clutch size in the Song Sparrows of the Pacific coast increases along a rather regular gradient from 3.05 in Baja California to 4.17 in Alaska (Johnston, 1954). This agrees with Lack's (1947) generalization that clutch size tends to increase from the tropics toward the poles. Another general trend is that when a female raises two broods in a single season, the second clutch is smaller than the first.

There is obviously an upper limit to the number of eggs a

female can lay, and to the number of young that can be raised successfully. In several species it has been shown that the average weight of nestlings is lower in large broods than in small ones. This could be important when the young leave the nest, as mortality in underweight young just out of the nest could be greater than in those of normal weight.

We must not forget that the female has a considerable investment of energy in the clutch. If this investment is too great she may not be as efficient in carrying out nesting duties. It is not likely that the flicker that laid 71 eggs in 73 days could have coped very efficiently with the demands of nesting. It has also been suggested that the size of broods is adapted to prevent excessive loss or gain of heat by the young in the nest.

At any rate, the idea that birds that suffer high nest mortality have large clutches and large broods as opposed to species that have low nest mortality is far too simple. More work needs to be done on nearly all aspects of this difficult subject. An excellent review of the ultimate factors affecting clutch size in birds has been written by von Haartman (1971). Those with some biological background would profit by reading this.

Nest Parasitism

Of considerable interest are those species known variously as *brood, nest,* or *social parasites.* They build no nest of their own but lay their eggs in the nests of other species, the young being reared by the foster parents, often to the detriment of their own offspring. The host species suffers because the brood parasite removes a host egg or eggs as she lays her own. Further, since many of the species parasitized are smaller than the parasite, and since the development of the foster young is often more rapid than that of the host's nestlings, the stranger is usually the largest of the brood and receives an inordinate share of the food brought by the parents.

In the United States the most common brood parasite is the Brown-headed Cowbird, a fairly common summer bird of the

Monterey Bay area. Cowbirds usually lay a single egg in the host's nest, an individual distributing the eggs of her clutch among several nests. However, nests with five or more cowbird eggs have been reported (Mayfield, 1965; Elliot, 1977). In such cases, undoubtedly more than one female was involved. In California the average female lays 24 eggs each breeding season (Payne, 1976).

Birds parasitized by the cowbird have three defenses. They may eject the cowbird's egg from the nest; built a second nest on top of the first, thereby burying the cowbird's egg(s) and any of their own that may have been laid; or simply abandon the nest and start anew elsewhere. Obviously, the first method is the most efficient.

Rothstein (1975) introduced a single artificial cowbird egg into each of 640 nests of 43 species of birds, nearly all passerines. He removed a single egg of the host at the time he introduced the artificial egg. The 30 species for which he had adequate data fell into two classes, "accepters" (23) and "rejecters" (7). There was little intraspecific variation; all, or nearly all, the individuals of a given species responded in the same way. Eighty percent of the rejections involved ejection, the most efficient response.

The effect of brood parasitism on the host species varies greatly from one species to another. Nice (1937) found that it had a moderate effect, at best, on the population of Song Sparrows which she studied. On the other hand, the cowbird is a serious, possibly the most serious, enemy of the Kirtland's Warbler, an endangered species which breeds only in a restricted area in Michigan (Mayfield, 1961; Walkinshaw, 1972; Anderson and Storer, 1976). The continued existence of this species has been threatened by the cowbird, which invaded its range recently, probably since 1890 (Mayfield, 1961). Available data suggest that the cowbird is also a serious parasite on the Golden-cheeked Warbler, which has a restricted breeding range in south-central Texas (Pulich, 1976).

Often the effects are local, correlating with local increase in numbers of the cowbird. Grinnell and Miller (1944) noted that there had been a noticable decline in the numbers of the Bell's Vireo, a heavily parasitized host species, in some parts of southern California and the Sacramento and San Joaquin valleys, apparently as cowbird numbers built up. The late Walter I. Allen told one of us (Davis) that the Blue-gray Gnatcatcher, once common near Altadena, California, had been locally exterminated by cowbird parasitism.

Eggs

Eggs, of course, come in all sizes, shapes, and colors. Some are unmarked; others may be marked with a variety of speckles, dots, lines, scrawls, and blotches. The ground color, if any, is added during the process of shell formation, and surface markings are added as the egg moves down the oviduct after the shell has been completed. Pigment is deposited on the shell surface by pigment glands in the oviduct. If the egg is stationary, a speckle, dot, or blotch results. If the egg is moving down the oviduct without rotation, a line results. If it is moving and rotating, a scrawl results.

Because eggs are so varied in color and pattern, and many are of great beauty, egg collecting was at one time a popular hobby. Those who participated were known as oologists, and a number of journals, all long defunct, were devoted to this "science." W. Leon Dawson, author of *The Birds of California,* even founded "The Museum of Comparative Oology" in Santa Barbara in 1919. It wambled through two dreary years before joining the Passenger Pigeon and the Great Auk. Egg collecting is much restricted today and is done by ornithologists, under permit, when needed to find the answers to specific questions, not as a pastime.

Lack (1958) made a detailed study of the colors and patterns of the eggs of the thrushes, a very large and widely distributed family. Some of the generalizations he made apply to many kinds of birds other than thrushes. He found that egg color is useless as a guide to the classification of birds but is associated with the nest sites typical of a given species. Hole nesters tend to have white eggs. This is probably to make the eggs more visible to the adults. Particular ground colors and patterns are associated with particular nest sites (on the ground, on ledges, in bushes or trees, or in domed nests), presumably affording some degree of concealment to the eggs in these various situations.

Incubation

After the completion of the clutch, incubation, the covering of the eggs by a parent, begins. This keeps the eggs at an even temperature and one high enough for proper development of the embryo to the hatching stage. In most species this activity is carried out by the female; in some, by both parents, with the female usually carrying most of the load; in a handful of species, by the male alone.

As we noted under "Reproduction," most species of birds develop a bare area on the abdomen shortly before the start of incubation, the *incubation* (or *brood*) *patch*. This allows bare skin to be applied directly to the eggs, thus greatly assisting the transfer of heat from the parent. Since the female usually does most or all of the incubating, it is not surprising that females almost routinely develop a brood patch. The occurrence of such patches in males seems to be random. Some species in which the male regularly performs part of the incubation, such as the Bushtit and the Black-headed Grosbeak, lack them, whereas they have been found in occasional males of some species of flycatchers in which the female performs all the incubation. In the phalaropes, in which the male alone incubates, males have incubation patches and females do not. In Montana the Clark's Nutcracker nests from February to April, when temperatures are frequently at or below freezing. The eggs are covered 99.5 percent of the time, the male performs 20 percent of the incubation, and most nesting males have well-developed incubation patches that are of obvious value (Mewaldt, 1952, 1956).

As Drent (1975) emphasizes, the eggs and the incubating parent should be thought of as a unit. If the body temperature of the parent rises or falls, the same will happen to the eggs. Thus, the parent must keep its own body temperature constant. If air temperature falls rapidly the incubating bird may shiver or take other measures to produce more heat; if it rises rapidly the parent may pant or respond in other ways to lower its body temperature. Experimental work, mainly with chickens, indicates that optimal incubation temperatures have a very narrow range and that prolonged exposure of the eggs to temperatures only a few degrees above or below this range will cause either abnormal development or death of the embryo.

The development of the embryo involves many physico-chemical reactions which are influenced by temperature. Among those that have been measured are the rate of water loss from the egg and the rates of gas exchange through the egg shell. This last has a great effect on the relative proportions of oxygen and carbon dioxide present within the egg. Before hatching the average egg loses 18 percent of its initial weight as a result of water loss (Rahn and Ar, 1974). Incubation is far more than the simple "plunking down" of a parent on the eggs. It represents a very intricate and delicate relationship among the eggs, the structure and porosity of their shells, the nature of the nest, ambient temperatures, and the behavior of the incubating parent. The latter must maintain its own body temperature within narrow limits and must behaviorally regulate the intensity of incubation. This can be done by varying the amounts of time spent on and off the eggs and by adjusting the closeness of the contact between the incubation patch and the eggs. The incubating parent may frequently adjust its position to bring about a desired degree of contact. Turning of the eggs by the incubating bird is often seen. This helps to maintain an even egg temperature.

Hatching

Hatching is also a complicated process. Its success depends largely on the young bird's being in a proper position within the egg. This is brought about partly by the turning of the eggs during incubation and mainly by a series of complicated movements made by the young bird inside the egg.

Escape from the shell is aided by the *egg tooth,* found in most, if not all, families of birds. This is a rather sharp projection at the end of the upper mandible. In a few species there are two egg teeth, one on each mandible. At hatching the egg tooth is driven through the shell near the blunt end, a process known as *pipping.* This is aided by the *hatching muscle* on the nape. After the egg tooth has penetrated the shell, the embryo rotates counterclockwise, thus cutting the cap off the egg and making an escape route. The egg tooth either falls off a few days after hatching or it disappears gradually. The hatching muscle becomes much reduced in size.

Although the hatching of a clutch may be spread over a day or more, the eggs usually hatch within a short period. In part, this happens because heavy incubation does not start until the last or next to last egg has been laid. In addition, the embryos within the eggs make audible clicking sounds as hatching time approaches. These are apparently produced by respiratory movements. This communication among the embryos has been shown experimentally to be important in synchronizing their hatching (Vince, 1969).

The Young

The stage of development reached by the young at hatching depends on the species involved. *Precocial* young, characteristic of loons, grebes, galliform birds (fowl, quail, grouse, turkeys, and others), rails, and shorebirds, among others, are well covered with natal down at hatching. They are quite active and leave the nest shortly after their down dries. Most precocial young follow the parents and get their own food. *Altricial* young hatch naked or with sparse, patchy down. Their eyes are closed, they cannot stand erect, and about the only coordinated movement of which they are capable is raising the head and gaping for food. Such young are entirely dependent on the parents and spend an appreciable period in the nest. They are characteristic of hummingbirds, kingfishers, woodpeckers, passerines, and others.

Birds that leave the nest soon after hatching are called *nidifugous* ("nest fleeing") and those that spend an appreciable amount of time in the nest are called *nidicolous* ("nest inhabiting"). Between the extremes of precocial and nidifugous on the one hand, and altricial and nidicolous on the other, there are intermediate stages characteristic of various bird groups. Gulls and terns, for example, hatch with a heavy coat of down but they spend a few days in the nest. Skutch (1976) recognizes five classes of newly hatched young, and the reader is referred to his opus for details.

Development of the altricial young of most species is rather rapid. The eyes open within a few days, and muscular movements become more varied and better coordinated. As we noted previously, weight, a good indicator of overall size, increases at a tremendous rate. This is made possible in part by the disproportionate development of the digestive system in the embryo. This gives newly hatched altricial young a grossly "pot-bellied" appearance. The enormously developed digestive system enables the young to handle efficiently the great amounts of food brought by the parents. The ensheathed feathers of the juvenal plumage begin to appear within a few days. The degree of development of this plumage when the young bird leaves the nest depends mostly on the length of the nestling period.

At hatching most birds cannot control their body temperature. This is true of the precocial young of many species as well as of altricial young, and this is why young chickens and quail must be brooded by a parent at night. At this stage metabolic rate fluctuates with air temperature. As ambient temperature rises, metabolic rate increases; as it lowers, metabolic rate decreases. This is exactly the opposite of what occurs in mature birds.

Most altricial young achieve a high degree of *thermoregulation* (ability to control the body temperature by controlling heat loss) between seven and 14 days. The age at which a young altricial bird can first thermoregulate depends primarily on its growth rate (Dunn, 1975) and secondarily on the length of its nestling period (Ricklefs and Hainsworth, 1968). If the young of two species have the same growth rate but different nestling periods, the young with the longer nestling period will achieve thermoregulation later. It was formerly believed that the ability to thermoregulate depended almost entirely on the development of the juvenal plumage as an insulating layer. This is a great oversimplification; plumage development is only one of several factors involved and perhaps not the most important one at that.

Dawson and Evans (1960) list the following factors as important in achieving thermoregulation by nestling Vesper Sparrows. As the nestlings grow, the proportion of body surface to body mass declines so that there is relatively less skin through which heat is lost. As muscles develop and as muscular coordination increases with continued development of the nervous system, the ability to produce heat by active movements increases. Of special importance is the ability to produce heat by shivering. The heart and liver increase in size and development more rapidly than do most other internal organs, so that there is a rapid increase in circulatory efficiency and liver function. Finally, continuing growth of the juvenal plumage provides better insulation. This last is by no means the most important factor; nestling Field and Chipping sparrows achieve a fair degree of thermoregulation before the feathers of the juvenal plumage start to break out of their sheaths (Dawson and Evans, 1957).

Another aid to thermoregulation is behavioral. By huddling in the nest, the young effectively reduce the ratio of exposed surface to mass and cut down heat loss. The placement and insulating qualities of the nest are also important in the timing of thermoregulation in the young.

Care of Nestlings

Feeding the nestlings is usually done by both parents. In those "lek" species that have altricial young, and in hummingbirds, the female does all the feeding. Although there is great interspecific variation in feeding rate, in general food is delivered to the young more frequently as they grow.

In some species, nest sanitation is maintained faithfully by the parents; they carry the droppings of the young some distance from the nest and discard them. In other species adequate sanitation is maintained by the parents for only a few days. After this the young, now capable of active movement, back up to the rim of the nest and expel their droppings. Many fail to clear the nest and adhere to the outside surface, which is well plastered with droppings by the time the young depart. House Finch nests are typical of such "nest fouling" species.

The young of most species are cared for by the parents after they have left the nest and until they are capable of living independently. In most of the altricial birds of the Monterey Bay area the young are fed and otherwise helped by the parents for a period of two to three weeks outside the nest. The gradual breakup of families of the Western Flycatcher (Davis et al, 1963) is perhaps typical of most of our small passerines. The young flycatchers observed in this study tended to stay close together in the first few days out of the nest, flying only short distances. After the fifth to the seventh day, flight became longer; between the seventh and ninth days, the young made their first successful hawking flights to capture flying insects. Up to this point they had been fed entirely by the parents, but after this they began to do more and more of their own foraging. Gradually the amount of food supplied by the parents decreased, and by the time the young had been out of the nest between two and three weeks, feeding by the parents ceased altogether. In this period the young became increasingly independent of each other and of the parents. There was a gradual lessening of the cohesion of the family group and in most cases, within three weeks after the young had left the nest, the members of the family had dispersed. In no instance was a parent seen to attack or attempt to drive any young bird away, although this has been reported in some species.

After the young of the last brood have dispersed, the breeding season ends for the pair of adults involved. Their activities from this point on will depend on their status as residents or migrants, on whether they pair for life, and on the nature of their defended territory—permanent or breeding season territory only. For our resident birds this is a quiet period, individuals simply maintaining themselves through the molt, free of the arduous duties of the breeding cycle.

7

MOLTS AND PLUMAGES

THE POSSESSION OF FEATHERS sets birds apart from all other animals. These marvelously designed structures perform a number of vital functions. They provide the major organs of flight (the wings and tail), superb insulation against heat and cold, and a tough, resilient protective coat; and they give birds the sleek, streamlined contour necessary for efficient flight. In addition, most of the visible colors and patterns of birds depend on the pigmentation and/or structure of their exposed feathers.

Since a fully grown feather is a dead structure, it cannot be repaired if damaged. Therefore the plumage (here taken to mean the total feather coat), subjected to the wear and tear of ordinary activity and to the extreme wear of nesting, becomes much worn down or abraded, and certain colors eventually become much faded as a result of exposure to light. There must be some mechanism designed to provide periodic renewal of the plumage before it becomes so worn and, in some cases, so faded as well that it can no longer carry out its functions.

Such periodic renewal is accomplished by a series of replacements in which old feathers are lost and their places taken by new ones. Each such change is called a molt, and the process of feather replacement is called molting. A complete molt involves all of the plumage; an incomplete molt, only part of it. Normally, birds replace their plumage once a year by a complete molt. In many species there are two molts a year, one complete, the other nearly always incomplete. Molts occur in a definite sequence, and each molt and the succeeding plumage have definite names.

Ventral views of a female Acorn Woodpecker collected on 24 February 1976 *(left)* and a male collected on 9 July 1976 *(right)*. By July, the pointed tips of the tail feathers of the male had been worn away in the course of normal activity. (R. Buchsbaum)

There is no aspect of ornithology more controversial than molting. There are two different sets of names in use for molts and plumages, one based on Dwight (1900), the other on Humphrey and Parkes (1959). Each has its advocates, and both terminologies appear in the literature. Even words such as "plumage" (used in this discussion in the *Webster's International Dictionary* sense, "the entire clothing of feathers of a bird") mean different things to different people. The matter is much complicated by the great variation found among birds in the timing, rate, extent, and sequence of molts. Such variation is not only interspecific, but may even be intraspecific.

A good example of this is found in the White-crowned Sparrow. Nearly all young birds of the subspecies *gambelii* and *pugetensis* molt the head feathers just before their first breeding season, losing their dusky and brown head striping and acquiring black and white striping similar to that of adult birds. Most young birds of the race *nuttalli* of the central coast of California, however, do not have such a head molt and breed in the subdued head striping of their winter plumage (Blanchard, 1941; Michener and Michener, 1943). A detailed discussion of the complexities of molting is out of place here. Rather, we should think in terms of what molting does and what it means to birds in terms of their entire annual cycle.

At hatching, young birds wear a plumage composed of very soft, fluffy "natal down." In some young birds (ducks, quail, shorebirds, gulls, and many others) down covers the entire head and body. In others, most notably the songbirds, the down is very sparse and restricted to a few parts of the head and body. The young of some birds, such as kingfishers and most woodpeckers, hatch naked. Down is shed in the nest by young which spend a long time there, and outside the nest by young which leave shortly after hatching.

The succeeding plumage is softer and fluffier than that of adults except for wings and tail, which are usually nearly similar to those of adults. The softer head and body plumage is advantageous for young that spend some time in the nest, as its compressibility allows the young to huddle more efficiently. The wing and tail feathers are usually only partly grown when the young leave the nest. The sight of stubby-winged, bob-tailed young following the parents is common in spring and summer.

Although soft, lacy plumage may have been advantageous in the nest, it does not wear well. It is not surprising, then, that young birds molt in late summer or early fall and replace this plumage with one that resembles adult plumage in texture and firmness. In the young of many species, however, some of the wing feathers and some or all of the tail feathers are not lost at this molt. They are quite similar to those of adults and are not worn down much by autumn.

Adults undergo a complete molt after the breeding season, losing the worn, faded feathers, most or all of which they have carried for a year, and replacing them with fresh ones.

The next molt, which is not found in all species, occurs just before the breeding season and is nearly always incomplete. Changes in color and/or patterns are often involved, especially in males. A good example of this molt is found in the American Goldfinch, the males of which lose the brown head and body feathers of the winter plumage and replace them with black feathers on the forehead and bright yellow feathers elsewhere. This is also the molt at which young White-crowns of certain subspecies acquire black and white head stripes.

Some species acquire bright plumage just before the breeding season without molting at all. In the male Blue Grosbeak, for example, in fresh fall plumage the blue feathers of the head and body have broad edgings of buff or brownish. Since the feathers overlap, much of the blue is obscured. By the breeding season, however, these edgings have worn off and the male assumes his characteristic rich blue coloration. Similar changes occur in some other species.

Again at the end of the breeding season, adults replace all of the plumage; and young of the year, coming into their first winter, replace all or most of the plumage, depending on species. And so the cycle of feather replacement continues through the life of the individual.

The physiological control of molt is extremely complicated and, again, there is great interspecific variation. Hormones produced by the thyroid, the gonads, and the pituitary all seem to be important to varying degrees in controlling the onset and end of various molts and the rate of feather development. Although much experimentation has been carried out, the results, sometimes in the same species, are often contradictory. Research thus far has pointed out a number of promising lines to follow but it has given us few definite answers.

As with reproduction, there is a question of when molting would best occur in the annual cycle. Here we are concerned primarily with the major molt which occurs in late summer or early fall. Molt is an energy-consuming process, and the metabolic rate of molting songbirds ranges from 5 to 30 percent above normal. Since developing feathers are richly supplied with blood, it is also possible that there is greater opportunity for loss of body heat, especially at low temperatures (King and Farner, 1961). The increased metabolic rates during molt may be the result of increased heat production to maintain body temperature.

There is also a nutritional demand made on the molting bird, although this is not nearly as great as that made on the laying female. Feathers are composed almost entirely of keratin, a protein material, and the plumage accounts for a moderate proportion of the bird's total weight. For example, in the Steller's Jays of central coastal California, the plumage in spring accounts for about 8 percent of body weight and the fresh plumage following the fall molt, about 10 percent (Pitelka, 1958).

As was true of reproduction, the major molt of the year, at which time all or nearly all of the plumage is replaced, should occur at a time of year when temperatures are relatively high and insects easily available. One might ask why molt and reproduction do not occur at the same time. As Payne (1972) states, the energy requirements of molt, although less than those of breeding, if added to breeding requirements might mean the difference between successful and unsuccessful nesting. If these two activities occurred one after the other, the breeding effort would not be endangered. The warm months from spring through early fall, with their favorable conditions, provide a period long enough for our resident birds, at least, to carry out breeding and molt in sequence.

Our migratory summer visitors face a more difficult problem because migration also requires a great deal of energy. Therefore, events must be timed so that neither breeding nor migration overlaps too extensively with the period of heavy molt. Since birds do not all migrate over the same distance at the same rate, it is not surprising that there is some interspecific variation in timing of molt relative to fall migration. Orange-crowned Warblers, for example, go through most or all of their molt before leaving for the south (Foster, 1967), whereas the Western Flycatcher goes through its fall molt on the wintering grounds (Johnson, 1974). In general, species which have a rapid migration defer the fall molt until they reach the wintering grounds, whereas birds which have a prolonged migration go through most or all of the molt before leaving (Johnson, 1963).

Birds of high latitudes have special problems in that they have a short season and most of them migrate rather early. Different species show different adaptations to this more rigorous schedule. The Gambel Sparrow near Fairbanks, Alaska, molts after the breeding season. The molt is rapid and highly synchronized in the population, with nearly all birds molting within the same limited period (Morton et al., 1969).

The sandpipers which breed at Point Barrow, Alaska, above the Arctic Circle, show different schedules, depending largely on the length of the migrations they must make to the wintering grounds. For those species which make a lengthy trip to a winter range below the Equator, early departure is advantageous and they postpone the fall molt until they arrive on the winter range.

The Red-backed Sandpiper, or Dunlin, however, winters from southern British Columbia south only to the State of Sonora, Mexico. This species starts to molt its flight feathers at the time of egg-laying. Molt proceeds slowly during the nesting season, and most of it occurs after breeding is over. The Dunlin stays on the tundra after the other sandpipers have left; in their absence there is little competition for food. It is during this long stay in the tundra region that molt is completed before the southward migration (Holmes, 1966).

As with reproduction, different schedules have evolved in different species according to the demands put on them. The relations among breeding, molt, and migration are a prime illustration of how the timing of important events in the annual cycle of a population has become adjusted so that each critical activity may be carried out successfully without disrupting any other.

8

MIGRATION

BIRD MIGRATION may be defined as the regular movement of birds between alternate areas occupied by them at different times of the year. One area is that in which the birds breed; the other is better suited to support them in the nonbreeding season. There is a great deal of variation among birds in the extent to which they are migratory.

Some species, such as the Brown Towhee and California Quail, are entirely resident. Others, such as the Olive-sided Flycatcher, are completely migratory; all members of the species move from the breeding range to a far distant winter range and return to the breeding area at the proper time in the next season. In species such as the Dark-eyed Junco and the White-crowned Sparrow, some subspecies are resident, others are strongly migratory. Storer (1951) showed that different populations of the same subspecies of Painted Bunting migrate to different wintering grounds, and Nice (1937) found that some individuals of a rather small Song Sparrow population were migratory and others were resident.

In some species, such as the Yellow-headed Blackbird, there is a general southward shift of the breeding population in fall and winter; this shift leaves a broad area of overlap between the breeding and winter ranges. In the eastern subspecies of the Yellow-bellied Sapsucker there is a migratory difference between the sexes; most females move farther south in winter than do most males (Howell, 1953). And in the west we even have a case of reverse migration. The Heermann's Gull breeds on islands adjacent to Baja California and the northwestern coast of mainland

Mexico. After the breeding season, some individuals stay in the breeding areas for the winter; others move as far south as Guatemala; and still others migrate *north* as far as Vancouver Island and winter commonly off the coasts of Oregon and California. The latter group migrates *south* to breed in the next season.

True migrations are different than *irruptions* of certain species of birds. The latter occur irregularly and usually involve northern or montane species in years when the food supply on which they depend for winter survival fails. Under these circumstances, large numbers of birds leave their normal range and wander far and wide in search of food. What proportion of such wanderers returns to the usual area to breed is not known. A good example of irruptions involves the invasions of Clark's Nutcrackers which occurred in many parts of California, including the Monterey Bay area, in the fall and winter of 1898-99, 1919-20, 1935-36, 1950-51, 1955-56, and 1961-62. At least the last two coincided with widespread failure of pine and fir cone crops in the Sierra Nevada (Davis and Williams, 1957, 1964). As a result, the birds were unable to store the conifer seeds on which they depend in winter. Cone crop data are lacking for other irruption years.

What are the *ultimate* factors in migration, those advantages which account for its evolution? Migration before the breeding season brings the individual (and the breeding population of which it will be a member) to a favorable area at a time of year when conditions are best for reproduction and subsequent molt. Conversely, migration after the breeding season returns the individual (and the other birds in the breeding population of which it was a member) to areas of favorable food supply and climate in which to pass the nonbreeding season. Competition may have also been important in the evolution of migration (Cox, 1968).

Research on migration focuses on four main topics. First, what are the *proximate* factors involved? Here we are dealing with the factors that are actually responsible for the timing of migrations. These would include physiological timing mechanisms and the environmental fluctuations to which they respond. Internal rhythms would also be considered here. Second, what are the physiological changes that a bird must make when it gets ready to migrate? Third, how do birds orient themselves properly and navigate on their lengthy migrations? Finally, what are the patterns of migration for a given species? The effects of weather on migrations are one of the prime targets of investigations included in this category. We shall consider only the first three questions.

Experimental work on migration has been made possible by a peculiar type of behavior displayed by birds which are ready to migrate but are confined in cages or aviaries. This is the so-called "migration restlessness," often referred to by its German name, *Zugunruhe.*

When birds are ready to migrate but are held captive, they show a pronounced restlessness, moving almost constantly for hours at a time, rarely perching for appreciable periods. Such behavior is invaluable to the research worker. First, it provides an easily detected sign that the captives have reached migratory condition. Thus, it is possible to confine birds in advance of their normal migration time and subject them to experimental routines to see if such manipulations accelerate, retard, or even suppress the onset of *Zugunruhe.* Such routines might involve the injection of hormones of various types, or the altering of daylength, artificially providing the captives with longer or shorter days, interrupted lighting schedules, and so on. In this way, information may be gained on the factors controlling the timing of migrations.

Second, invaluable information may be acquired on how birds orient and navigate, again taking advantage of *Zugunruhe.* A circular cage or aviary is provided with a number of perches. When captives show *Zugunruhe,* they fly from perch to perch, moving almost constantly for long periods. In experimental cages, each perch is fitted with a recording device. This often takes the form of an electrical switch which is closed whenever a bird lands. The current provided operates a pen or other marker which records the "hit" on a moving chart. It is then possible to

Activity orientation cage used at the Avian Biology Laboratory at California State University, San Jose. The 8 perches are arranged peripherally; each is attached to an arm, the other end of which pivots over a contact microswitch housed under a sheet-metal box. When a bird leaves a perch, depressing it, the switch is closed and the visit is recorded on a continuously moving tape (from Mewaldt, Morton, and Brown, 1964).

see which perches are being used most frequently in a given period of time.

If the cage or aviary is located so that the captives can see the sky, they will use those perches in that sector which is in line with the direction in which they would migrate if they were free. If the captives would normally be migrating to the northwest, they use the perches in the northwest sector of the cage. In other words, the birds orient their cage movements to the normal direction of migration.

One may then manipulate the conditions in which the cage is kept. It can be exposed to the sky or kept indoors and subjected to different photoperiods. For night migrants the cage can be taken into a planetarium and the captives can be shown different

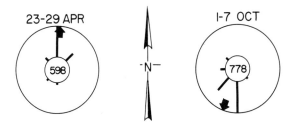

Diagrams of summed perch records for Gambel's White-crowned Sparrow for the nights of 23-29 April *(left)* and 1-7 October *(right)*. In April, when free-living birds would be migrating north, the perch records were clustered mainly in that sector of the cage. The opposite was true in October, when free-living birds were migrating south (from Mewaldt, Morton, and Brown, 1964).

star patterns to see how this affects the orientation of their *Zugunruhe.* There are many possibilities.

A simple but ingenious device for monitoring the orientation of *Zugunruhe* was developed by Emlen and Emlen (1966). This consists of a large funnel made of white blotting paper, supported by a metal pan. The lower end of the funnel rests on an inked pad. The experimental bird is introduced into the funnel and a wire screen is placed over the top to prevent its escape. A bird showing *Zugunruhe* will flutter to the top of the funnel, slide down, and land on the inked pad. Each time this happens, the bird leaves its track on the blotting paper. At the end of the experiment the tracks are examined to determine the directions of the attempted escapes. Birds in such funnels may be subjected to the same experimental routines as those previously mentioned. The disadvantages are that the tracks cannot be counted for time periods shorter than the total duration of the experiment, and only one bird at a time can be monitored.

The great amount of experimental work that has been done on all aspects of migration has produced a welter of results, and the interpretation of these findings is often difficult. The problem is complicated by the great amount of interspecific variation in critical features of migration. Another difficulty is that we are dealing with two quite different kinds of migration—one in the early spring before the breeding season and a second in late summer or early fall after the breeding season. The physiological states of birds are so different at these two points in the annual cycle that what we find out about one migration may not apply to the other.

Nonetheless, certain trends are evident in the masses of experimental data, and it is obvious that birds must reach a certain state of preparedness before they can migrate successfully. We may turn our attention to some general information that applies to what Farner (1955) calls "typical migrants." Most of the summer and winter visitant birds of the Monterey Bay area fall into that category.

Since migration demands a great deal of energy, it is not surprising that birds store energy before starting their journeys. This is stored in the form of fat deposits which occur in many places in the body. Deposits under the skin (subcutaneous deposits) are readily visible when a bird is examined in the hand, and one can estimate rather accurately the total fat content of the individual by the degree of development of these visible accumulations. In species such as the Dark-eyed Junco, the migratory races deposit fat heavily before migrating, but the resident races do not show such accumulations at any time.

The stored energy is not enough for the entire journey, and birds must stop from time to time and feed heavily to replenish their depleted fat reserves. At one station in the USSR it was found that when migrating birds with large subcutaneous fat deposits arrived they stayed only a short time, whereas lean birds stayed several days and put on considerable weight (Dolnik and Blyumenthal, 1967).

Birds which migrate overland and can stop frequently to replenish their fat stores put on only moderate amounts of fat. Birds whose migration route includes a long flight over water or unfavorable terrain, such as a desert, load very heavily with fat before embarking on this lengthy passage. Cases of such migrants which have been investigated in detail indicate that they have ample stores of fat to support the long, sustained flights which they must make, with considerable reserves left over (Johnston and McFarlane, 1967; Odum et al., 1961).

However, birds which must make long desert flights in hot weather cannot store water, and they are not physiologically adapted to the high temperatures which they must face. Undoubtedly, many perish. Miller and Stebbins (1964) noted a number of severely stressed, dying, or dead migrants in late summer in the Joshua Tree National Monument of southern California. Warblers and small flycatchers seemed to be the most seriously affected.

The accumulation of fat in migratory birds is the result of a sharply increased intake of food prior to migration. This change in feeding habits is known as *hyperphagia,* and it bears no resemblance whatsoever to overeating in humans, which is commonly a neurotic response to psychological stress of some sort. Since hyperphagia occurs shortly before the spring and fall migrations, increased food intake comes at times when temperatures are relatively high and there is no great demand for energy to maintain body temperature. As a result, more food (=fuel) is taken in than is used up, and fat is deposited. The rate of accumulation is high, and a small bird may store an adequate supply in only a few days.

Accompanying fat deposition there is a change in metabolic activity, and species which have been metabolizing mainly carbohydrates shift to metabolism of fats as migration approaches (Dolnik and Blyumenthal, 1967). This is obviously necessary if migrants are to make use of the fat reserves which they have stored.

In many species of birds, experimental studies have indicated that, for the spring migration at least, the photoperiodic cycle is of great importance in bringing the individual into a migratory state. Indeed, the classic experiments of Rowan which we discussed under "Reproduction" were carried out mainly to test the effect of photoperiod on the timing of migration. The effects of long days on the testes was "fallout" from work designed to test another hypothesis. Not only did Rowan's experimental juncos show great development of the testes, but when light-treated birds were released, many were never seen again. On the other hand, the controls stayed in the immediate vicinity of the aviary after release. Rowan assumed that the experimental birds had embarked on a northward migration far ahead of time. He later repeated these experiments with Common Crows and achieved somewhat similar results.

Wolfson (1942) repeated Rowan's experiments using resident and migratory subspecies of the Dark-eyed Junco. Birds of both types were exposed to long days starting about mid-December at Berkeley, California. They were marked and released well before the normal time for migrant juncos to leave for the north. Resident birds deposited no fat and remained near the aviary when released. Migratory birds deposited fat heavily and most of them disappeared when freed. One of the migrant experimentals was captured at Redding, California, 320 km north of Berkeley, on 10 February, 10 days after release.

A great deal of work has been done subsequently on the effects of photoperiod on migration. At present it appears that the photoperiodic cycle is of primary importance in bringing most "typical migrants" to a state of migratory readiness in spring. The role of photoperiod in the fall migration is much more speculative. It is also unsatisfactory as an explanation for the northward migration of North Temperate species which winter on or near the Equator, where days are of even, or nearly even, length throughout the year; and for birds such as the Pectoral Sandpiper and Bank Swallow which winter mainly south of the Equator, where seasons are reversed.

As with reproduction, experimental evidence suggests that in some species, perhaps many, there is an internal rhythm of preparation for migration that is kept in time by the photoperiodic cycle. How widespread such a system may be among birds is not known. But, as in reproduction, the role of daylength is of major importance either as a direct stimulating agent or in keeping the timing of an internal rhythm precise so that fat deposition, onset of *Zugunruhe*, and necessary metabolic adjustments occur at the proper time in the annual cycle. What the physiological mechanism is that responds to increasing daylength as a factor in migration is not known at present.

Finally, we may consider orientation and navigation by migrating birds. This is a fascinating but highly technical subject and we shall consider it in a rather general way. As Emlen (1975) has noted, modern investigators have abandoned the idea that a given species uses only one particular method of navigation which depends on one particular kind of information. Rather, a given species may use several methods of directing flight, each dependent on a different type of information. There may be a preferred, or usual, method, but if the information needed to make it work is not available, a bird may resort to a quite different method if the necessary information for it is available. We may consider some of these different methods of navigation in broad detail. Readers with a technical background, especially those with some knowledge of physics, or of nautical or aeronautical navigation, should read Emlen's (1975) outstanding and fascinating review of the subject.

The navigational abilities of birds range all the way from short flights directed by the individual's familiarity with local landmarks to very long flights over strange terrain by birds transported to far distant, unfamiliar release points. A spectacular example of the latter involved the Laysan Albatross (Kenyon and Rice, 1958).

Eighteen Laysan Albatrosses were captured on their nests on Sand Island, Midway Atoll, tagged distinctively, and then taken by plane to remote release points. Fourteen returned to their nests, flying over vast stretches of open ocean. The long-distance champion returned 6600 km from the Philippines in 32.1 days. The speediest bird returned 5150 km from Whidby Island,

Washington, in 10.1 days, flying an average of 510 km daily. All returnees went to their nests. One bird was found badly injured the day after release and three were never seen again. Several had been released outside the species range and could not have been familiar with the release points. These included birds released at Whidby Island and the bird released in the Philippines. Obviously, the Laysan Albatross has spectacular navigational ability.

There are three major kinds of information which can be used for flight direction. First, there are visible landmarks. Known landmarks are obviously useful for short flights. They may also be useful in guiding a bird to a precise spot after a long flight. The Laysan Albatrosses, after their long journeys, undoubtedly zeroed in on their nesting colony and found their nests by using this kind of information. On longer flights, landmarks such as rivers, mountain ranges, and coastlines may provide directional aids enabling birds to keep on course.

Second, there are celestial clues such as the sun, the moon, and the stars. Daytime migrants can direct their flights by using their own position relative to the sun. This is not nearly as simple as it sounds because the sun moves across the sky as time passes. This means that a bird using the sun as a directional aid must keep changing its angle to the moving sun or it would steadily drift farther and farther off course if it maintained the same angle. Therefore, a bird navigating by the sun must have an accurate sense of time of day in order to compensate properly when the sun is in a particular position relative to it.

The demonstration by the late Gustav Kramer (1950, 1951) that captive Starlings showing *Zugunruhe* directed their activities in the proper direction for migration by keeping the proper angle to the sun was hailed as one of the major biological discoveries of the time. Kramer found that when the sky was overcast *Zugunruhe* became diffuse and undirected. If he used mirrors to change the angle of incidence of the sun visible to the birds, they shifted the direction of their movements accordingly. Since

Zugunruhe was maintained in the proper direction for hours at a time, it was evident that the birds had a built-in time sense and could compensate steadily for the sun's passage.

Night migrants apparently use stars or star patterns to direct their flights. This has been indicated by exposing caged migrants showing *Zugunruhe* to different night skies in planetariums. In such experiments, if the position of stellar north is reversed, the birds will shift the orientation of *Zugunruhe* by 180°, and if the dome of the planetarium is illuminated by dim, diffuse light, *Zugunruhe* either becomes random or ceases entirely (Sauer, 1957; Emlen, 1967a).

Two main methods of star navigation have been proposed. In one, birds presumably have a built-in time sense that enables them to use a particular star or constellation just as daytime migrants use the sun, keeping a proper angle to the reference point regardless of time of night. As Emlen (1975) notes, this would be much more difficult than solar navigation since the visible stars are not the same throughout the night or at different times of year; further, the night sky differs from the daytime sky in which there is a *single* prominent celestial clue, the sun, which is present at all times of the day and year. However, some experiments, especially those carried out by E.G.F. and E.M Sauer in Germany, do suggest that some night-migrating species have a built-in time sense that enables them to navigate by keeping a proper angle to a stellar reference point that is shifting.

On the other hand, Dr. S. T. Emlen of Cornell University has carried out planetarium experiments which indicate that some species tell direction by means of *fixed star patterns;* this would not require a time sense (Emlen, 1967a, 1967b). Emlen subjected Indigo Buntings showing *Zugunruhe* to manipulated sky patterns which should have thrown them "off course" if they had been relying on an internal timer to keep them oriented properly. But the buntings kept "on course." Emlen noted that *patterns of stars* are fixed and serve to indicate direction at any time of night, even though the stars themselves may be moving across the sky. For

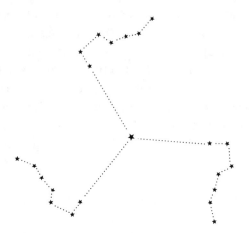

The fixed relationship between the Big Dipper and Polaris, the North Star.
Although stars "wheel" across the night sky, this relationship does not change.
Such fixed star patterns may be one source of directional information for night-
flying migrants.

example, the North Star is in line with the two stars that form the
outside wall of the cup of the Big Dipper. If one follows the line
that passes through these two stars from the bottom of the cup to
the top, his eye will be led to the North Star at any time of night.
Therefore one may find north by using this *star pattern* without
knowing time of night. Emlen hypothesized that some night
migrants, at least, navigate in this fashion.

Finally, we may consider the earth's magnetic field as a source
of navigational information. Detection of, and response to, magnetic lines of force could be a powerful aid to navigation. This
idea was first proposed seriously by H. L. Yeagley (1947), a
physics professor at Pennsylvania State University. He carried
out a series of experiments on homing pigeons which suggested
that his experimental birds were depending at least in part on
lines of force from the earth's magnetic field. His experiments
were criticized severely, especially by other physicists, and
further experiments led to conflicting results. As a result, the idea
of geomagnetism as a factor in bird navigation was dropped for
many years.

More recently, however, the possibility of magnetic orientation has become of interest again. In a number of cases birds have become disoriented by magnetic fields produced by man-made installations. Southern (1975) found that Ring-billed Gull chicks which oriented to the southeast under normal conditions oriented in random fashion when exposed to the magnetic field produced by the U.S. Navy's "Project Sanguine" communication system, and Larkin and Sutherland (1977) found that radar-tracked migrants flying over Project Sanguine (now called Project Seafarer) either changed direction or altitude when the antenna system was operating. Recently, small deposits of magnetite, a naturally magnetic material, have been found in a small area between the skull and the outer brain membrane in homing pigeons (Walcott et al., 1979).

Experimental work by W. Wiltschko and his colleagues in Germany, W.T. Keeton and his group at Cornell, and C. Walcott and his co-workers at SUNY at Stony Brook suggests strongly that geomagnetism is important to bird navigation. Much work is ongoing, and the future will see exciting discoveries in this aspect, and indeed in all aspects, of bird navigation.

9

THE BIRD YEAR—ANOTHER VERSION

THE FIRST HALF OF SEPTEMBER is the quietest part of the bird year at Hastings Reservation. Summer visitors have left for southern wintering grounds and the winter visitants have not yet arrived. Most resident birds have completed the annual molt or are in its final stages. Males are in a state of gonadal inactivity although by the end of the month a few males of a few species may sing occasionally. They are either adults which have passed through the refractory period or, more likely, early hatched birds of the year which have never before been sexually active. In either case they are responding to the still-long days of late summer. Since daylength is decreasing, this response will not last long. Bushtits and the resident juncos are forming flocks, and families of quail are grouping together in coveys.

In the last half of September the first winter visitants appear. Some of the newly arrived crown sparrows sing occasionally, suggesting low-level activity of the interstitial tissue of some males. Banding records indicate that many of these early arrivals do not stay in the area for long; they are probably individuals refueling briefly before moving farther south.

In October flocks of crown sparrows and juncos continue to build up as more migrants come in to stay. Residents that hold permanent territories, such as the Wrentit and Brown Towhee, are more tolerant of intruders and may allow unattached conspecifics to use their areas. For most of the ground foragers, seeds form the greater part of the diet. Seeds are in good supply in late summer and early fall. With the onset of winter rains in October and November, a substantial part of the seed supply germinates and is converted to a form which is of limited usefulness to most seed-eating birds. The Golden-crowns, however, feed extensively on newly sprouted annuals in addition to seeds and benefit greatly from the abundance of new, green plant material. Competition among the other seed eaters is undoubtedly intensified at this time.

By November the winter picture has largely stabilized. All winter species have arrived and those birds that defend winter territories have settled on them. Winter flocks have also settled in certain areas and, except for periods of stormy weather or a rare snowfall, few new birds are recorded in the banding area.

In the last half of January we detect the first signs of the new breeding cycle. Some passerines sing at low intensity, the song bouts short and infrequent, the songs of low volume and often shorter than usual. Nonetheless, these songs are the first indication to the field observer that the testis cycle has started its active phase in a few males. Rufous-sided Towhees, Dark-eyed Juncos, and Bewick's Wrens are among the first species to start singing. The juncos are undoubtedly residents; when residents and migrants of the same species winter together, gonadal activity starts earlier in the former.

January and February are months of stress for seedeaters. This is well before the seeding out of annual grasses in May and June which accounts for most of the seed supply. At this time the individuals at the lower end of the dominance hierarchies in winter flocks of seedeaters undoubtedly suffer severe stress, as shown by Fretwell (1968, 1969). The Golden-crowns, taking advantage of the abundant supply of annuals, would not be stressed as much as would juncos and White-crowns. In the last half of February the willows along streamcourses start to set flowers, and some of the seedeaters, especially juncos, augment their diets with nutritious catkins.

In February the Golden-crowns and Puget Sound and Gambel's white-crowns start an incomplete molt which lasts in most individuals until their departure in April. In this molt immature White-crowns acquire their black-and-white crowns;

the head stripes of Golden-crowns become longer and darker and the gold stripe between them becomes brighter.

In February and March gonadal activity progresses in the resident males, and singing and territorial behavior become more prominent. A few pairs of some species may nest in late February. Flocks of Bushtits have largely broken into pairs, and some of these may have started to build nests. In March more species begin to nest. Flocks of House Finches have broken up and California Quail start to pair up in their coveys.

March also marks the arrival of most of the summer visitant species. The preponderance of insectivores is very noticeable in these breeding season visitors: Poor-will, Western Kingbird, Ash-throated, Western, and Olive-sided flycatchers, Western Wood Pewee, Violet-green Swallow, House Wren, Blue-gray Gnatcatcher, Solitary and Warbling vireos, Orange-crowned, Yellow, and Black-throated Gray warblers, and Northern Oriole. Such birds as Black-headed Grosbeaks and Chipping Sparrows are in large part insect eaters in spring and summer. In addition, resident species such as the Rufous-sided and Brown towhees, Lark Sparrows, and Dark-eyed Juncos, normally vegetarian in winter, eat a large amount of insect material in spring and summer (Martin et al., 1961). Since large numbers of vegetarians such as crown and Fox sparrows and migrant juncos leave in spring, there is a decided switch from a bird fauna mainly dependent on vegetable material to one mainly dependent on arthropods.

As soon as the summer visitants arrive, the males go about the business of establishing territories and attracting mates. Their singing and other territorial behavior are very prominent in this period but become much less so as pairs are formed and settle down.

In April the winter visitants depart for northern breeding grounds. These migrants gain weight or show large amounts of fat as they prepare for their northward migration. This has been shown in Dark-eyed Juncos (Wolfson, 1940), Golden-crowned and Fox sparrows (Linsdale and Sumner, 1934), and Puget Sound and Gambel's white-crowns (Blanchard, 1941; Blanchard and Erickson, 1949) and undoubtedly is true of our other winter visitants before they depart. By April the gonad cycle has progressed in these migrants to the point at which many males are singing before departure.

Many birds start their nesting in the last half of April. The breeding season ends for most pairs by mid- to late July, and the gonads regress rapidly. Song, save for occasional early-morning singing, is infrequent and most birds are quiet and not much in evidence. Resident birds start their annual molt at the end of the breeding season. This molt is complete in adults and in birds of the year in some species; in some species it is incomplete in the young of the year. Migrants may or may not molt, depending on the timing and length of their migrations. By late August most of the summer visitants have departed on their southward migration. In the first half of September occasional transients from farther north pass through. The arrival of the first winter visitants signals the beginning of a new bird year.

10

THE EFFECTS OF DEVELOPMENT ON BIRD LIFE

GORDON (1977) has reviewed many of the changes that have occurred in the avifauna of the Monterey Bay area as a result of human activity. We are concerned here primarily with the effects of urban and suburban development on our birds. The coastal and foothill sections of Santa Cruz and Monterey counties have been subjected to intense development pressure in the past two decades, pressure which apparently will continue indefinitely. Considerable acreage has been converted from natural habitats supporting a wide variety of native birds into housing developments, shopping centers, golf courses, tennis clubs, and the like. What are the effects of such human-caused changes on the bird populations which were originally present?

A few studies have been made of the avifaunas of residential areas in the United States. Woolfenden and Rohwer (1969a) analyzed the bird populations of three suburban areas near St. Petersburg and Gulfport, Pinellas County, Florida. They found that the older the suburb the greater the density of breeding birds. In new residential suburbs they estimated density at 200 pairs of breeding birds per 40 hectares (100 acres), and in "mature" suburbs at 500 to 600 pairs per 40 hectares. Eleven species bred in the study areas, but four—the Mourning Dove, Blue Jay, Mockingbird, and House Sparrow—made up over 90 percent of the total. House Sparrows alone represented about 50 percent of the breeding birds.

Woolfenden and Rohwer (1969b) also analyzed breeding-bird populations in two natural woodlands near St. Petersburg.

Species diversity was similar: 12 species were present in the woodlands and 11 in the suburbs. Average density was lower— 121 breeding pairs per 40 hectares. Mockingbirds and House Sparrows were absent in the natural areas.

Emlen (1974) compared the birds present on 35 hectares of a residential area in Tucson, Arizona, with those of a desert area 16 km away. The desert area was chosen because it closely resembled the residential area before development, as shown in old photographs. He found that the density of birds was 26 times as high in the urban area as on the desert—1,230 versus 47 birds per 40 hectares. Species diversity was lower, with 14 species present in the residential area and 21 in the desert. Sixty-five percent of the urban birds belonged to three "invader" species already accustomed to urban conditions before they arrived. One, the Inca Dove, expanded its range north from Mexico starting about 1870. The other two, the Starling and the House Sparrow, were exotic species which spread west from sites of introduction on the eastern seaboard. None of the three occurred in the desert area. The House Sparrow accounted for 42 percent of the urban bird population. Other birds which increased greatly in the residential area were native species, especially the White-winged Dove and the House Finch. The last two had densities 280 and 510 times as high, respectively, as in the desert.

Most of the increase in the urban area was accounted for by seedeating species. Emlen (1974) found that residents there were putting out about 7 kg of bird seed, scratch feed, and table scraps daily at feeding stations. Assuming a feeding rate for seedeaters of 25 percent of body weight per day, these handouts would have supplied half of their daily needs.

Gavareski (1976) studied the diversity of bird species in city parks in Seattle, Washington. A large natural area was used as a control. In a large city park where the natural vegetation had been allowed to remain, species diversity was comparable to that in the control area. The smaller the park, or the more exotic the vegetation, the lower was the species diversity. A small park with greatly modified vegetation had the lowest species diversity and the greatest proportion of "city" birds. A census of breeding bird populations in cemeteries in central Chicago showed that the larger the cemetery, the greater the number of species found (Lussenhop, 1977). Such information is valuable when parks or greenbelts are established in or near developments.

Guth (1979) made a series of censuses of breeding birds along a transect in the Chicago metropolitan area. He found a total of 51 species. Five species accounted for 85 percent of the individuals counted, the House Sparrow, Starling, Common Grackle, American Robin, and Rock Dove, in order of decreasing abundance. There was greater species diversity in the suburbs than in the inner city, and the extent of tree canopy and size of yard were the two most important factors involved.

The general picture that emerges from these studies is that the residential development of an area leads rapidly to a great increase in the numbers of birds present, some decrease in species diversity, and a virtual takeover of the area by a handful of species which thrive in human-disturbed situations. Unfortunately, these dominant species include such exotics as the Rock Dove, Starling, and House Sparrow.

The success of these city species derives in part from their taking advantage of the many roosting and nest sites afforded by buildings, plantings, utility poles and wires, and the like. Undoubtedly a very important factor is their tolerance of human disturbance. Foot and automobile traffic, wandering dogs and cats, car horns and other city sounds are apparently tolerated by relatively few bird species. The inevitable increase in the number of domestic and feral housecats, efficient predators on birds, works to eliminate ground nesters.

What species in our area thrive in disturbed situations? The inevitable trio of exotics—Rock Doves, Starlings, and House Sparrows—is certainly to be expected as invaders following development, as are a few native species. House Finches and Brewer's Blackbirds are common in developed areas. Mockingbirds and American Robins are quick to establish as soon as suitable plantings are present. American Coots in fall and winter often congregate about ponds and inlets adjacent to grassy areas. They are often a nuisance, cropping and fouling lawns and driving other species away. Coots have been controlled in the past around El Estero by the City of Monterey, around artificial ponds on at least one resort area in the Carmel Valley, and on the Naval Postgraduate School golf course because of their undesirable behavior.

In short, it seems inevitable that where there is suburban development we may expect a great increase in the numbers of birds, some loss of species diversity, and the takeover of the local avifauna by a handful of exotics and aggressive native species tolerant of human disturbance.

11

BIRD HABITATS

Introduction

IF WE CONSIDER the entire assemblage of land birds found in the Monterey Bay area, it is obvious that each species occurs in a particular kind of habitat or, more frequently, in two or more habitats with one preferred over the other(s). For example, in our area oak woodland is the first choice of Acorn Woodpeckers, Scrub Jays, and Plain Titmice, although they occur in other habitat types as well. If we classify each bird according to its habitat preferences, we may divide our avifauna into groups, each made up of species with either an exclusive or primary preference for a particular habitat.

The exact grouping will depend largely on the scheme of habitat classification we adopt. Considering all the vegetational and physical features of our area, we may make out a number of *habitat types.* Physical features such as sea cliffs, lakes, and rivers offer no problems; they are self-defining. Vegetational habitat units offer more alternatives. They may be defined broadly according to the life form of the predominant vegetation. Examples are forest, woodland, and scrub. Such categories are, in most cases, too broad to be useful. They may be broken down further according to the dominant plant species present. Examples are oak woodland, redwood forest, and chamise chaparral. If our classification is fine enough, we find that each habitat type supports a characteristic group of birds.

The species which occur in a given habitat use it in different ways. For example, in the breeding season Nuttall's Woodpeckers, White-breasted Nuthatches, and Blue-gray Gnat-catchers are common in blue oak woodland. The woodpeckers dig out insects and insect larvae from the bark, the nuthatches glean insects from the surfaces of trunks and main limbs, and the gnatcatchers glean insects from the foliage. Each bird thus occupies a distinctive *niche* within the oak woodland. If a habitat is a bird's address, its niche is its profession, usually defined in terms of food-gathering. The reader interested in more information on the niche and its relation to interspecific competition should read the very lucid and readable paper by Diamond (1978), based almost entirely on examples drawn from birds.

The pioneer, and still the best, classification of California's breeding birds according to habitat was made by Miller (1951). He carefully described a number of vegetational and physical habitats and drew up lists of all the breeding bird species found in each. More importantly, he rated the preference of each species for each habitat in which it occurred. For example, the Chestnut-backed Chickadee was listed as occurring in oak woodland, but also noted is the fact that this habitat is its third preference, the primary preference being coastal forest, the secondary, riparian woodland. Some birds were considered to have an exclusive preference for a single habitat, as the Western Meadowlark for grassland. Some, such as the Great Horned Owl, were listed in as many as 11 different habitats, with oak woodland most preferred, chaparral least. Miller's meticulously done work made a path for others to follow. More recent workers (Brown et al., 1973; Small, 1974) have listed the birds of man-made habitats not included by Miller.

We have chosen to define our vegetational habitats mainly on the basis of Thorne's (1976) *The Vascular Plant Communities of California.* It must be understood, however, that the words "community" and "communities" present problems of definition. Botanists tend to use "community" to denote a group of plants occupying a particular area and having coincident or overlapping physical requirements. The group is defined in terms of its dominant species. Such communities are descriptive and not functional although they are very useful.

To the ecologist, however, a community is composed of populations of organisms which occupy a particular area and are *interdependent*. Such a community is functional rather than purely descriptive. Interdependence may take many forms, including competition, predation, and parasitism. Sometimes interdependence is easily seen. Acorn Woodpeckers depend on oaks for food and for food storage sites, Plain Titmice are dependent in part on old woodpecker holes for nest sites, and oak regeneration depends partly on acorns buried by Scrub Jays for future use. Often the interrelationships among the member populations of a functional community are very difficult to work out. Biologists who view the community as a functional unit may use such words as "association" or "formation" for the vegetational units often termed "communities" by botanists.

Where two different plant communities meet, a given species of bird may use both. Usually there is a rather gradual transition between two communities, leading to the presence of an intermediate zone, or *ecotone,* containing elements of both. The variety of bird species is often higher in such ecotonal situations as they may be occupied by many of the birds found in both of the plant communities involved. Some species of birds may actually be restricted to ecotonal situations.

Less commonly, the two vegetation types meet abruptly with the formation of a sharp edge between the two. Again, bird species diversity is often higher in such "edge" situations, and a given species may use the communities forming the edge in different ways. For example, the California Quail is often an "edge" species, using grassland for foraging and sometimes for nesting but using immediately adjacent brush or tree cover for refuge and roosting.

In the following accounts, the lists of birds which we give as being characteristic of the various inland habitats of our area include only breeding species. Winter visitants and transients are

An old hayfield at the Hastings Reservation. On the left there is a sharp *edge* between grassland and riparian vegetation, mainly willows. On the right there is an *edge* between grassland and the lower edge of Mixed Evergreen Forest. Such habitat is ideal for California Quail, Rufous-sided and Brown towhees, and winter flocks of Dark-eyed Juncos and Golden-crowned Sparrows. (R. Buchsbaum)

included only for marsh, shore, and aquatic habitats. Some species may appear under more than one heading. Although they may prefer a particular habitat, they may occur commonly in others as well.

Oak or Foothill Woodland

OAK WOODLAND, or foothill woodland as it is also called, in our area is found almost entirely east of the crests of the Santa Cruz and Santa Lucia mountains. The oaks are of particular importance in this community. The blue oak dominates much of the woodland; the valley oak is also common and widespread.

The coast live oak, very important in mixed evergreen forest near the coast, is much more restricted and scattered in the foothill woodland. Interior live oak is common in the woodland of the Santa Cruz Mountains but not in Monterey County. Canyon live oak and black oak, included by Miller (1951) in his "oak wood-land" formation and by Small (1974) in his "oak woodland," are more properly considered components of the mixed evergreen forest.

The digger pine, a common associate of the blue oak over much of California's Foothill Woodland, occurs in a few res-tricted areas east of the crest of the Santa Cruz Mountains. It is found in a few places in Monterey County, but not in our area.

In the upper Carmel Valley and its adjacent foothills, foothill woodland lies between the open grassland below and the oak-madrone phase of the mixed evergreen forest above (Griffin, 1974). A detailed description of this woodland, strongly domi-nated by blue oaks, has been given by White (1966); he gives much information on the sizes, spacing, life forms, and densities of the trees involved.

In aspect, oak woodland varies from areas of closely spaced, small trees to a parkland of widely spaced, large trees. The cover beneath the oaks is mainly grassy and herbaceous. The woodland is often somewhat patchy, interrupted by areas of grass and/or brush. Frequently, relatively continuous oak woodland may con-tain grassy clearings which are important because they create local "edge" effects. Sometimes such clearings are related to changes in soil type. In other cases they result from one oak's outstripping its fellows and reaching large size. The extensive crown of such a tree shades out other oaks, and when one of these large trees finally dies, it either topples or slowly decomposes in a clearing of its own making.

Sometimes the oaks form a parklike savanna of widely spaced, large trees separated by expanses of grassland. Typically, the understory is grassy. Some consider oak savanna a mixture of plant communities rather than a distinct community (e.g., Miller,

Blue oak woodland at Hastings Reservation. The trees are small and closely spaced; the understory is mainly grassy. (K.L. White)

Savanna form of blue oak woodland, with moderately large trees, widely spaced. (K.L. White)

1951), but it is better regarded as a phase of foothill woodland (Munz, 1963; Thorne, 1976; Griffin, 1977). Near the coast, coast live oaks are involved in such savannas, which are transitional between mixed evergreen forest and foothill woodland. Inland, savannas occur typically on valley floors; blue oaks, and to a lesser degree valley oaks and coast live oaks, are involved. In the Santa Lucias, valley oak savannas occur at high elevations within the mixed evergreen forest (Griffin, 1976).

The failure of blue oaks and especially of valley oaks to regenerate in our area has been reported by White (1966) and Griffin (1971, 1973, 1976). This is an interesting story and deserves some discussion here.

As is well known, some birds and mammals eat acorns, thus reducing the supply available for regeneration. In addition, certain mammals eat oak seedlings or browse them repeatedly, either retarding their growth indefinitely or eventually killing them (Linsdale and Tomich, 1953; Griffin, 1971, 1976). On the other hand, Grinnell (1936) pointed out that those birds and mammals which store acorns in the ground for future use act as planters. Many stored acorns are not retrieved and may germinate, thus aiding regeneration or even bringing about marginal extension of oak woodland.

In a survey of the vertebrates most importantly affecting oak regeneration at the Hastings Reservation, Griffin (1976) found that the Acorn Woodpecker, Yellow-billed Magpie, Scrub Jay, pocket gopher, and mule deer were the major consumers of acorns; the gopher and deer were the most important eaters of, and browsers on, seedlings; and the jay and magpie were the most important planters. On adjacent ranches, cattle were major consumers and browsers. To this list we may add, for other parts of our area, the Band-tailed Pigeon as a major consumer and the Steller's Jay as a major consumer and planter. The introduced wild boar may also be important locally as a consumer.

The most important factor operating against oak regeneration is the seedling destruction caused by browsers and certain insects

A huge, dead blue oak, slowly decomposing in a grassy clearing of its own making. The closely spaced, small blue oaks of the adjacent woodland are visible in the background. Such large trees often used by American Kestrels and Western Bluebirds. (K.L. White)

Foothill vegetation on the Hastings Reservation showing nearly unbroken chamise chaparral (**A**) and oak savanna (**B**). (R. Buchsbaum)

(Griffin, 1976). Seedlings that are browsed repeatedly fail to grow and eventually die. Coast live oak seedlings are more resistant to persistent browsing than are the seedlings of blue and valley oaks. Some may reach the sapling stage and escape further setback. Griffin (1971) noted that of one group of 17 coast live oak seedlings recorded at Hastings in 1940, eight survived repeated browsing and by 1969 were becoming saplings, finally escaping from the deer after nearly 30 years. The failure of blue and valley oaks to regenerate may result in the conversion of some oak savannas to grassland or from blue and/or valley oak savannas to coast live oak savannas. Where adjacent to mixed evergreen forest, valley oak savannas may be invaded by Coulter pines, canyon and interior live oaks, and tanoaks (Griffin, 1976).

Oak woodland supports a large variety of birds in our area. Not only do the oaks themselves provide a large number of nest sites, shelters, and roosts, but they also provide abundant food. Acorns, of course, immediately come to mind. One species, the Acorn Woodpecker, is a specialist on acorns and is famous for the large granaries in which it stores these nuts. Stores are usually placed in large trees, the successive generations of woodpeckers inhabiting a particular area drilling hundreds or thousands of holes in the bark over the years, harvesting acorns as soon as they are available in the fall and storing them in the snug receptacles which they have made. When the acorn crop is good, such stores will carry a group of birds through the winter and at least until the following spring, when they rely in large part on insects for food. Near the coast, coast live oaks provide most of the acorns, but the bark of these trees is too wet to provide good storage holes, and the woodpeckers usually locate their granaries in pines or in wooden power poles. Farther inland, large valley oaks are most favored, followed by blue oaks and sycamores. The complex behavior of Acorn Woodpeckers, centered on the defense and use of such stores, has been described in detail by MacRoberts and MacRoberts (1976), based on their extensive field observations made at the Hastings Reservation.

Perhaps it should be emphasized here that the Acorn Wood-peckers *do not,* as the old myth would have it, store acorns to attract insect larvae on which the birds feed. The woodpeckers eat *the acorns, "wormy" or not,* and mast is the food on which they depend over much of the year.

Jays and magpies, as previously noted, bury many acorns and use them throughout the fall and winter. Beal (1910) reported that 42.5 percent of the Steller's Jay's diet over the whole year is mast from acorns, with this food making up 85 percent of the diet from October to January. Corresponding figures for the Scrub Jay are 38 percent for the year and 74 percent from October to January.

In addition to woodpeckers, magpies, and jays, which can open sound acorns, many other kinds of birds eat acorns which are damaged or broken so that the meats are exposed. Sometimes birds may take advantage of acorns opened by other animals. At the Hastings Reservation, Brown and Rufous-sided towhees have been seen to eat bits of mast adhering to pieces of husk spit out by deer. One observer watched a Scrub Jay as it shelled an acorn. A Plain Titmouse, a Rufous-sided Towhee, and two Brown Towhees stayed within four feet of the jay and when it flew carrying the acorn, the other birds followed it.

Conversely, Linsdale and Tomich (1953) noted that Acorn Woodpeckers, Yellow-billed Magpies, and especially Scrub Jays harvesting acorns at Hastings dropped many nuts and also clusters of leaves which came away with twigs when acorns were pulled free. Nuts and leaves were eaten eagerly by the deer waiting below, and deer tended to congregate under trees in which these birds were harvesting.

In addition, leaf buds and staminate catkins of coast live, blue, and valley oaks are eaten by a variety of birds. The two deciduous oaks are also parasitized by mistletoe, and the berries are eaten by many species of birds in winter, especially by the Western Bluebird. Grinnell and Storer (1924) described the way in which this species swallows the mistletoe berries whole, digests the skin and part of the sticky, gelatinous layer surrounding the seed, and defecates the seeds still encased in a thin layer of this sticky material. If defecation occurs while a bird is perched in an oak, the seeds adhere to twigs and branches and await germination. Thus, the birds are a major agent in the transport of mistletoe from tree to tree. The Western Bluebird, American Robin, and Cedar Waxwing are probably the major feeders on mistletoe berries in our area. Fence posts, trough edges, and other spots on which bluebirds perch become coated with adhering mistletoe seeds. Sutton (1951) described a similar role for a number of Mexican bird species in mistletoe dissemination.

The oaks also provide abundant leaf litter and humus which trap seeds and also provide living places for many insects and other arthropods. Brown and Rufous-sided towhees and wintering Fox Sparrows spend much time scratching vigorously in oak leaf litter and humus to uncover food items.

The large and varied insect fauna which the oak woodland harbors is of the greatest importance to many birds. This is especially true in the spring and summer when many of our seed-eating winter species are replaced by insectivorous birds; but even in winter this woodland is an important source of insects for many kinds of birds.

Species resident in the oak woodland are the Cooper's Hawk, Sharp-shinned Hawk, California Quail, Mourning Dove, Screech Owl, Great Horned Owl, Common Flicker, Acorn Woodpecker, Nuttall's Woodpecker, Scrub Jay, Yellow-billed Magpie, Common Crow, Plain Titmouse, Bushtit, White-breasted Nuthatch, Western Bluebird, Hutton's Vireo, Rufous-sided Towhee, and Brown Towhee. Summer visitants are the Ash-throated Flycatcher, Violet-green Swallow, House Wren, Blue-grey Gnatcatcher, Black-throated Gray Warbler, Lawrence's Goldfinch, and Chipping Sparrow.

Where the woodland assumes the form of a savanna, the avifauna is more restricted. Residents include the Red-tailed Hawk, American Kestrel, Mourning Dove, Great Horned Owl,

Yellow-billed Magpie, Common Crow, Western Bluebird, Starling, Brewer's Blackbird, House Finch, Lesser Goldfinch, and Lark Sparrow. In summer the Turkey Vulture, Western Kingbird, and Northern Oriole are also present.

Riparian Woodland

In many parts of the Monterey Bay area, riparian (streamside) woodland borders permanent streams, and intermittent streams if the water table is high enough. Common tree species in this community are red and white alders, black cottonwoods, California sycamores, bigleaf maples, and California boxelders. Willows are also an important component of this woodland. Some, such as the red willow, are good-sized trees; others, such as the arroyo and sandbar willows, are either large shrubs or small trees, and they may form dense thickets. Coast live oaks and valley oaks are sometimes intermingled with the other species.

A dense understory is often present, composed mainly of several species of currants and gooseberries, California wild rose, Pacific blackberry, and western creek dogwood, in various combinations.

Riparian woodland usually forms a rather narrow strip bordering stream courses, but where the floodplain is broad, as along parts of the Salinas River, it can be fairly extensive. Small (1974) has written an excellent account of the general characteristics and annual cycle of riparian woodland in California, and readers wanting further details should consult this.

Although riparian woodland is very restricted in extent compared to most other plant communities in our area, it is unusually attractive to birds and supports a large variety of species. As Miller (1951) notes, riparian woodland provides many edge situations as it contacts a variety of other communities. Further, he points out that most Californian vegetation types are adapted to dry conditions, and riparian woodland provides the summer-

Riparian vegetation, mainly willows and black cottonwoods, along the lower Carmel River. View downstream from the Highway 1 bridge. (R. Buchsbaum)

time shade and availability of surface water on which many species of birds depend in that season.

The resident birds of our riparian woodland include two hawks of great beauty, the White-tailed Kite and the Red-shouldered Hawk. Both were much reduced in numbers a few decades ago but in recent years both have made encouraging recoveries. This is suggested by the records of these species at the Hastings Reservation. Linsdale (1947) noted that in the first ten years of the Reservation's existence (1937-1947), there was only one record of the Red-shouldered Hawk and four of the White-tailed Kite. In the period 1966-1976, there was at least one pair of Red-shouldered Hawks present almost continuously (probably not the same birds throughout) and at least five observed nestings. Kites have been recorded for varying periods in each year and at least three nestings have been noted, two successful. The recovery of these two species has not been confined to our area but has occurred over most of their ranges in California.

Their preferred habitat includes riparian woodland adjacent to areas of open grassland where foraging, especially for small mammals, is carried out. The kite is almost a specialist on the California vole, a small grassland rodent belonging to the same subfamily as the lemming. Stendell and Myers (1973) studied the food habits of kites on the Hastings Reservation by identifying teeth and skull parts of small rodents contained in pellets of undigestible material cast up by kites at roosts and nests. They found that although the density of voles in the grassland at Hastings, as determined by live-trapping, was 12, 22, and ½ per hectare in 1969, 1970, and 1971, respectively, voles made up 83 percent, 84 percent, and 88 percent of the kites' diets in those years. Rather than seek new areas or shift to more common small rodents in 1971, when voles were very scarce, the local kites apparently increased their hunting efforts to maintain their high consumption of their preferred prey.

Species resident in our riparian woodland are the White-tailed Kite, Red-shouldered Hawk, Mourning Dove, Screech Owl, Long-eared Owl, Belted Kingfisher, Common Flicker, Hairy Woodpecker, Downy Woodpecker, Nuttall's Woodpecker, Black Phoebe, Chestnut-backed Chickadee, Bewick's Wren, American Robin, Brown-headed Cowbird, and Purple Finch. Summer visitors are the Black-chinned Hummingbird, Western Flycatcher, Tree Swallow, Purple Martin, House Wren, Swainson's Thrush, Warbling Vireo, Orange-crowned Warbler, Yellow Warbler, MacGillivray's Warbler, Yellow-breasted Chat, Wilson's Warbler, and Black-headed Grosbeak. The rather large number of summer visitors suggests the attractiveness of riparian habitat to birds in the hot part of the year, as noted by Miller (1951).

Coastal Closed-cone Coniferous Woodland

Coastal closed-cone coniferous woodland (Thorne, 1976) is one of the communities included by Miller (1951) in his "Coastal

Forest" formation and by Small (1974) in his "Coastal Coniferous Forests." Although termed "woodland" by Thorne, this community often forms a true forest. On the central coast of
California it is found only in three restricted areas. The northernmost lies between Año Nuevo Point, San Mateo County, and
Swanton, Santa Cruz County. The southernmost is near Cam-
bria, San Luis Obispo County. Between them lies the best-
developed stand, in the Monterey Peninsula-Carmel-Point
Lobos area.

Coastal closed-cone coniferous forest, Point Lobos. The "layered" trees in
the foreground are Monterey cypresses, and the tall trees in the background are
Monterey pines. Between them is a mixture of the two. (R. Buchsbaum)

This community was originally composed of four species of
trees: Monterey pine, bishop pine, Monterey cypress, and Gowen
cypress. The northern and southern stands of this woodland now
contain only Monterey pine but all four species occur in the
Monterey Peninsula area. Monterey pine is widespread; Monterey cypress occurs in two small areas along the rocky coast; and

one small stand of bishop pines and two small stands of Gowen cypress occur a short distance inland. Bishop pine is found from Humboldt County south to Santa Barbara County and on Santa Cruz and Santa Rosa islands, but the two cypresses are found only in our area.

Associated with our closed-cone woodland are the coast live oak and a variety of shrubs which occur in various combinations, sometimes as an understory in the woodland, sometimes adjacent to it. These include poison-oak, several species of manzanita and ceanothus, huckleberry, salal, spreading snowberry, northern sticky monkey-flower, and Pacific blackberry (Howitt, 1972; Vogl et al., 1977).

There is fossil evidence that this community and the birds associated with it formerly occurred much farther south. Miller (1932) reported on bird fossils collected from an asphalt pit at Carpinteria, on the coast about 10 miles southeast of Santa Barbara. Paleobotanists had previously identified fossils of Monterey and bishop pines, coast live oak, manzanita, and ceanothus from this pit. These plant fossils have recently been dated by Carbon-14 as occurring over 38,000 years ago (Warter, 1976). Among the bird species represented were Steller's Jay, a chickadee not certainly identified as to species but probably the Chestnut-backed Chickadee, Red-breasted and Pigmy nuthatches, and Red Crossbills. Some of these might be found today near Carpinteria where humans have planted conifers, but none is found there in habitat unaltered by man. The jay, chickadee, and Pigmy Nuthatch are common residents today of our closed-cone woodland, and the Red-breasted Nuthatch and crossbill are occasional winter visitants there. The key species is the Pigmy Nuthatch; as Grinnell and Miller (1944) note, the combined range of bishop and Monterey pines "coincides remarkably well" with the range of the coastal subspecies of the Pigmy Nuthatch. This is easily seen if one compares the map of Pigmy Nuthatch distribution in Grinnell and Miller (1944:320, fig. 29) with the distribution maps of bishop and Monterey pines in Griffin and

Critchfield (1972:86, 88, maps 52 and 55). Other fossils identified by Miller included those of the Wrentit and Rufous-sided Towhee. Both are common today in the shrubby vegetation associated with the closed-cone woodland.

Recently Warter (1976) reported the discovery in the Rancho La Brea tar pits in Los Angeles of a single bishop pine cone, many Monterey cypress cones, and a few cones of the Gowen cypress. These remains have been Carbon-14 dated as occurring 40,000 to 25,000 years ago and are comparable in age to the Carpinteria material. This makes it clear that closed-cone woodland similar to ours occurred in the Los Angeles area at one time, and undoubtedly a characteristic avifauna was associated with it. Trees and birds retreated to the north as climate changed.

Birds resident in this community in our area include the Sharp-shinned Hawk, Cooper's Hawk, Band-tailed Pigeon, Great Horned Owl, Pigmy Owl, Anna's Hummingbird, Common Flicker, Hairy Woodpecker, Steller's Jay, Chestnut-backed Chickadee, Bushtit, Pigmy Nuthatch, Brown Creeper, Hermit Thrush, Purple Finch, Pine Siskin, and Dark-eyed Junco. Summer visitors are the Allen's Hummingbird, Western Flycatcher, and Olive-sided Flycatcher.

Redwood Forest

The great redwood forest of northwestern California reaches its southern limit in Santa Cruz County. In Monterey County it has been reduced to outlying stands occupying steep, fog-dampened coastal canyons. A clump of redwoods discovered by James R. Griffin 2.4 km north of Salmon Creek, not far north of the San Luis Obispo County line, marks the absolute southern limit of redwood distribution as presently known. Redwoods rarely reach the coast proper but are nearly always separated from it by a rather narrow zone of other vegetation types. They may occur far inland, however, and in the Santa Lucia Mountains they have been recorded at 1,100 m elevation (Griffin and Critchfield, 1972).

A stand of redwoods on the University of California, Santa Cruz campus. Farther south, such stands are confined to fog-dampened coastal canyons.

In Santa Cruz County, Douglas fir is commonly associated with redwoods but it is of very limited occurrence in Monterey County. Other trees found with redwoods in our area are tanoak, California laurel, and coast and interior live oaks. Tanoak and madrone often form a forest on the dry edges of the redwoods (Thorne, 1976). Understory shrubs in the Santa Cruz County redwood forest include huckleberry, salal, and thimbleberry. The understory in these forests in Monterey County is generally sparse and includes poison-oak, thimbleberry, and occasional shrubs derived from bordering communities.

As Orr (1942) notes, birds are scarce in pure or nearly pure stands of redwoods because suitable seed-producing plants are uncommon and the insect fauna is limited. Redwood seed itself is small and not useful to birds. Where redwoods are mixed with other trees, the bird fauna is more diverse. Because the composition of the redwood forests of our area is so variable, it is difficult to make a list of birds characteristic of this community. A few resident species are found in redwoods wherever they occur. These are the Steller's Jay, Chestnut-backed Chickadee, Brown Creeper, Hermit Thrush, Dark-eyed Junco, and the Winter Wren, which lives in dense tangles in the deepest, darkest parts of the redwood forest. Dippers are found along some of our coastal streams where they pass through the redwoods. The occurrence of the species on the following list depends mainly on the composition of the forest at a given locality. Resident are the Band-tailed Pigeon, Great Horned Owl, Pigmy Owl, Common Flicker, Acorn Woodpecker, Hairy Woodpecker, Purple Finch, and Pine Siskin. Summer visitants are Vaux's Swift, Western Flycatcher, Western Wood Pewee, Olive-sided Flycatcher, and Wilson's Warbler.

Mixed Evergreen Forest

MIXED EVERGREEN FOREST extends from the coast to the eastern part of our area, reaching high elevations in the Santa Cruz and Santa Lucia mountains. Although much of it is somewhat removed from the immediate Monterey Bay area, it is readily accessible from the west by roads and foot trails. This community is included, with others, in Miller's (1951) "coastal forest" formation and in Small's (1974) "coastal coniferous forests." In our area it is perhaps best regarded as a somewhat watered-down version of Thorne's (1976) northern mixed evergreen forest.

In the Santa Cruz Mountains this community "usually occurs

adjacent to redwood forests but on drier sites and generally in more inland areas" (Thomas, 1961). On the west slope of the Santa Lucias it occurs mainly above the coastal scrub and grassland belt, often just above or inland from the redwoods of coastal canyon bottoms and lower slopes. On the east slope it usually occurs above the foothill woodland.

Prominent trees in this community are tanoak, coast live oak, canyon live oak, madrone, and California laurel (California bay). Interior live oaks are a rather common component of the forest in the Santa Cruz Mountains but they are of more local occurrence farther south. Black oak may also be present locally.

In the Santa Cruz Mountains, Douglas fir is commonly found in the mixed evergreen forest. In the Santa Lucias, no conifer is associated with this community over most of its range, but in some areas the Coulter pine may be a common associate. The bristlecone (or Santa Lucia) fir is common where the forest is fire resistant (Griffin, 1975). This tree is a Santa Lucia Mountains endemic, that is, found there and nowhere else.

In some coastal areas the mixed evergreen forest is heavily dominated by coast live oaks which may form pure, or almost pure, stands. Such stands may be large and extend a considerable distance inland. In the Aromas area, for example, coast live oak may extend inland for nearly 16 km (Sawyer et al., 1977). In the Carmel Valley the last such stand is on Snivley's Ridge, about 13 km up the valley from Highway 1.

Common understory species are bracken, poison-oak, coffeeberry, cream bush, toyon, snowberry, and spreading snowberry.

Orr (1942) stated that the "woodland" of the Big Basin area of San Mateo and Santa Cruz counties, a habitat as defined by him closely equivalent to mixed evergreen forest, was the most productive habitat for birds of all those which he studied. He found that a number of species common in chaparral or in dense coniferous forest also occurred in the woodland. Mixed evergreen forest is one of the most productive communities in our area also. Orr (1942) suggested that the insect fauna in this habitat is larger than in any other and that this attracted large numbers of insectivorous birds.

The evergreen forest is also more mesic (moist) and generally cooler and shadier than more open vegetation types and, like riparian woodland, it is attractive to many breeding species in summer. In addition, such trees as oaks, madrones, and pines (where present) provide much food for birds as do such shrubs as poison-oak, coffeeberry, and toyon. Madrone berries are of much importance to a number of species, especially the Band-tailed Pigeon and the American Robin, and Ralph Gutiérrez reports that the crops of Mountain Quail are sometimes crammed with fallen madrone blossoms.

Birds resident in the Mixed Evergreen Forest include the Cooper's Hawk, Sharp-shinned Hawk, Mountain Quail, Band-tailed Pigeon, Great Horned Owl, Pigmy Owl, Spotted Owl, Saw-whet Owl, Anna's Hummingbird, Common Flicker, Acorn Woodpecker, Hairy Woodpecker, Steller's Jay, Scrub Jay, Chestnut-backed Chickadee, Brown Creeper, Bewick's Wren, American Robin, Hutton's Vireo, Purple Finch, Rufous-sided Towhee, and Dark-eyed Junco. Summer visitants are the Flammulated Owl, Western Flycatcher, Western Wood Pewee, Olive-sided Flycatcher, Solitary Vireo, Warbling Vireo, Orange-crowned Warbler, Black-throated Gray Warbler, and Western Tanager.

Two ornithological discoveries of great interest have been made in recent years in the evergreen forest of the Santa Lucias. The Flammulated Owl, a summer visitant in California, had never been reported from the southern Coast Ranges until Ron Branson and Bill Reese tape-recorded a calling individual on Chews Ridge, in the Ventana Wilderness Area of the Los Padres National Forest, on April 30, 1966. On the following evening Vern Yadon saw one at the same locality and on July 20, 1966, he collected a specimen, now in the Pacific Grove Museum of Natural History, on Junipero Serra Peak. He also recorded this species on Cone Peak.

Flammulated Owls have subsequently been recorded many times in the Santa Lucias, and the species is apparently a widely distributed breeding bird there, arriving in early spring and migrating south in late summer or early fall. Since the discovery of this owl in our area, many birders have made the "pilgrimage" to easily accessible Chews Ridge to add this species to their life lists.

The Spotted Owl was unrecorded in the south Coast Ranges for many years although expert "owlers" had searched seemingly suitable habitat for the species for many years. Finally, it was discovered by Ron Branson and Bob Black on the south fork of Devil's Creek, near Ojito Camp in the Los Padres National Forest, in October 1964. Since then a number of additional records have been made in the Santa Lucias, both in the ever-green forest of higher elevations and in coastal redwood canyons. These owls have now been recorded at least from near upper Robinson Canyon and Chews Ridge in the north to the vicinity of Ojito and Buckeye camps in the south. Duos, presumably mated pairs, have been seen in early April, in late June or early July, on 1 August, and in December, and a single bird was seen in December. Juveniles presumably of this species have been recorded from Grimes Canyon and Ventana Big Sur, a resort just south of Big Sur. These records indicate that the Spotted Owl is resident in the Santa Lucias and in the coastal canyons of Monterey County at least as far south as Buckeye Camp.

Scrub

SCRUB, as used here, is a general term based on the structure and appearance of vegetation rather than on the kinds of plants which compose it. A number of distinct plant communities are included in "scrub," but all are characterized by a predominance of shrubs of low or medium height, closely spaced, often with individual plants touching. Depending on the kinds of plants involved and their spacing, passage for a human through such

vegetation ranges from fairly easy to impossible. Not included is
the shaded, brushy understory vegetation of forest or woodland.

The kinds of birds that use the various plant communities
included in scrub are largely similar, and it is therefore convenient to include these different types of vegetation in a single
category. Some authors (e.g., Miller, 1951; Small, 1974) have
used the term "chaparral" as synonymous with scrub; however,
to most botanists chaparral refers to a distinct plant community
rather than to a generalized vegetation type.

Three distinct plant communities are included in our scrub:
chaparral, northern coastal scrub, and southern coastal scrub
(Thorne, 1976). Since our area lies between the main distributions of the two coastal scrub communities, elements of both are
present and their interrelations are very complex. It is more
convenient for us to include both in a single "coastal scrub" unit.

Chaparral is adapted to dry areas. The individual shrubs tend
to be tough, springy, and much branched. Human passage
through chaparral is almost always difficult and often impossible. The leaves of the shrubs are usually small and stiff; in
some species they are resinous. These leaf characters are
adaptations to reduce water loss. Most species are evergreen and
most are fire adapted. Some, such as chamise, sprout from root
crowns or burls after a fire has destroyed the structures above,
and the regrowth of mature plants is an important adjunct to
growth from seed after a burn. In a number of chaparral species
the seeds may lie dormant for years until the heat of a fire
stimulates germination.

The most important plants making up our chaparral are
chamise and several species of wild lilac or ceanothus. Several
kinds of manzanita are locally important.

Chamise often forms pure, or almost pure, stands, especially
on south- and east-facing slopes. Such stands are used by rather
few birds; the chamise leaves, which are tiny and needle shaped,
build up little or no litter and humus, and the ground beneath the
shrubs provides little food. Where such pure stands form an edge

with foothill woodland, so that oak leaves may drift down and build up some litter beneath the adjacent chamise, bird use is heavier. Chamise seed, however, is eagerly sought by some birds, especially by the Lesser and Lawrence's goldfinches (Linsdale, 1957).

Coastal scrub is found in typical form within a mile or so of the coast, although poorly developed patches are found inland as far as the Hastings Reservation (Griffin, 1974). On the steep, west slopes of the Santa Lucias, coastal scrub and grassland form a zone of mixed vegetation below the mixed evergreen forest. Important components of coastal scrub are California sagebrush, black sage, coyote brush, northern sticky monkey-flower, and farther inland, Santa Lucia sticky monkey-flower. A number of other species are either minor components of this vegetation or are closely associated with it. Some are important to birds.

Several shrubby species bear juicy fruits which are important in supplying fluid to birds in hot, dry inland areas such as the upper Carmel Valley in late summer and fall. Most important is the coffeeberry, widely distributed and bearing large fruits. Hollyleaf redberry is less important in this regard. Toyon and poison-oak provide food for many species in winter. The hard seeds of poison-oak, indigestible in themselves, are covered with a thin, waxy coat which is highly nutritious. Some birds, such as the Dark-eyed Junco and the Golden-crowned Sparrow, "mouth" each berry, scaling off and swallowing the waxy coat and dropping the hard seed. Others, such as the Common Flicker, Nuttall's Woodpecker, and California Thrasher, swallow the berries whole, digesting the waxy coat and later regurgitating or defecating the seeds (Beal, 1907, 1910, 1911). Such species may act as disseminators of this noxious plant.

Birds resident in the scrub of our area are the California Quail, Mountain Quail (in the chaparral of inland foothills), Roadrunner, Anna's Hummingbird, Scrub Jay, Bushtit, Wrentit, Bewick's Wren, California Thrasher, Rufous-sided Towhee, Brown Towhee, Rufous-crowned Sparrow, Sage Sparrow, and White-

Open grass forming a sharp *edge* with a narrow strip of blue oak woodland at Hastings Reservation. In the middle background the chamise chaparral (**A**) to the left of the Reservation's fence line (**B**) has been opened up by grazing and contrasts with the dense, ungrazed chamise (**C**) on the Reservation. (R. Buchsbaum)

A shoot of chamise showing the terminal flower heads and the small, needle-shaped leaves characteristic of this plant. The leaves, 4 to 10 mm long, build up little or no litter but the seeds are eagerly sought by some birds. (R. Buchsbaum)

Coastal scrub, mainly coyote brush and California sagebrush, at Point Lobos. (R. Buchsbaum)

crowned Sparrow (subspecies *nuttalli* resident in coastal scrub of the immediate coastal area). Summer visitants are the Poor-will, Allen's Hummingbird, Ash-throated Flycatcher, Blue-gray Gnatcatcher, Orange-crowned Warbler, Lazuli Bunting, and Black-chinned Sparrow.

An unusually large proportion of the songbirds resident in our scrub (the ten species from the Scrub Jay through the White-crowned Sparrow in the above list) have rather short, rounded wings and long tails. A measure of this is the wing/tail ratio (length of wing divided by length of tail). A ratio of 1.0 would indicate wing and tail of equal lengths, less than 1.0 would indicate tail longer than wing, and greater than 1.0, the reverse. Birds inhabiting dense, much-branched vegetation make rather short flights and tend toward short-wingedness. A long tail serves as a rudder, as a counterbalance when running, and it may also be used to assist a bird in climbing upward through brush.

Of the ten species considered here, seven have wing/tail ratios which range from 0.71 to 0.93. The other three species are the Bewick's Wren (1.01), the Sage Sparrow (1.01), and the White-crowned Sparrow (1.04). The Bewick's Wren, however, has the lowest wing/tail ratio of the seven species of wrens found in California, the other six ranging from 1.07 to 1.53. The White-crowned Sparrow is the only species of the ten which does not occupy dense chaparral in at least part of its local range. The Sage Sparrow seems to be the major exception to the rule.

Two of the ten species, the Wrentit and California Thrasher, are virtually confined to heavy brush. Small (1974) notes that Wrentits often refuse to cross firebreaks or trails cut through their brushy habitat. This species has the lowest wing/tail ratio of all (0.71). The thrasher not only occupies heavy brush but takes wing only in dire emergency, nearly always preferring to run, rather than fly, from disturbance. Engels (1940) also noted that the California Thrasher is "extremely agile" in climbing upward through brush and is aided importantly in this activity by the long tail, which is used as a lever. Its wing/tail ratio is 0.79. The next lowest is the Rufous-sided Towhee, with 0.86.

This tendency in our resident scrub birds is put into sharper relief if we compare them with the songbirds resident in the mixed evergreen forest (refer to for list of species). Only the Rufous-sided Towhee is common to both lists. The other seven forest species have wing/tail ratios which range from 1.04 (Brown Creeper) to 1.34 (Purple Finch).

Grassland

OF ALL the major vegetation types in California, the grasslands have changed most from their original condition as a result of human activities. Although no one may say definitely, most botanists and plant ecologists believe that the pristine Californian grasslands were dominated by perennial bunchgrasses. As humans colonized the state in the 18th and 19th centuries they introduced many exotic grasses, most importantly a variety of annuals from the Mediterranean region. They also introduced a number of forbs (nongrass herbs), many of which became prominent in the grasslands. And, along with man, came his cattle.

Under the impact of grazing—more accurately, overgrazing—the native bunchgrasses were reduced to more or less scattered remnants, and the more aggressive introduced annuals flourished and largely took over. The first appearance of these invaders in our area probably coincided with, or closely followed, the arrival of the Spanish in the latter part of the 18th century. Whether the introductions of exotics were accidental or purposeful no one knows; undoubtedly both kinds occurred. The entire character of the grasslands changed within a short period of time; by the middle of the 19th century, travelers to parts of Monterey County reported extensive areas grown to oats.

The degree of contamination of the original grasslands of our area is indicated in a rough way by the following. Howitt and Howell (1964) list 162 species of grasses occurring in Monterey County; 91 (56 percent) are native and 71 (44 percent) are introduced. Further, of the 12 largest families of plants (those with most species occurring in the county), the grass family has the largest percentage of introduced species. Thomas (1961), who included a larger number of escapes of restricted occurrence, recorded 95 introduced grasses (51 percent) and 91 native species (49 percent) in the Santa Cruz Mountains. Perhaps a more realistic picture is given by Griffin (1974), since his report pertains to the Hastings Reservation, an area well removed from population centers where unusually large numbers of escapes are found. Even here, only 29 species (51 percent) of the established local grasses are native and 28 (49 percent) are exotics.

A stand of purple needlegrass, one of the most important of the native perennial bunchgrasses, at the Hastings Reservation. The measuring stick is 1 m long. (K.L. White)

The impact of grazing on grassland. On the left of the fence is ungrazed grassland on the Hastings Reservation, on the right a heavily grazed pasture of an adjacent ranch. (K.L. White)

We have first-hand knowledge of the ease with which exotics may be accidentally introduced into a remote area. In the course of trapping and banding birds at Hastings, giraffe head, an exotic mint found only in a few restricted areas on the reservation, and broomcorn millet, an introduced grass never before recorded there, appeared near a number of bird traps. Both species were undoubtedly introduced into the trapping area from the chick scratch and wild bird seed used as bait.

The work of White (1967) indicates that, once exotic grasses have become established at the expense of the native perennials, the natives will return painfully slowly, if at all, even to an area which lies fallow, protected from grazing or any other human-caused disturbance. White compared small stands of purple needlegrass, one of the most important of the native bunch-

Grassland on the Hastings Reservation. The grassland in the foreground, from the lower edge of the photograph to the fence line, although ungrazed for over 40 years, is still composed almost entirely of introduced annuals. (R. Buchsbaum)

grasses, on areas at Hastings which had been protected for 27 years, with stands on lightly and moderately grazed land. The percentage of needlegrass cover and the mass weight (weight of oven-dried clippings) per unit area did not differ significantly between the protected and grazed stands.

Natives important in our grasslands include rye grass, perennial fescue, needlegrass, barley, melic grass, bluegrass, each represented by several species; and squirrel-tail. Important introduced grasses are oat, annual fescue, bromegrass, darnel or ryegrass, and barley, each represented by several species; and silver hairgrass. A number of forbs, native and exotic, occur in the grassland, and it is these forbs that provide the spectacular wildflower displays that are so characteristic of the Californian grasslands.

In addition to drastic changes in species composition, vast areas of pristine grasslands have been eliminated by agricultural activities. California's leading position as an agricultural state has been achieved mainly at the expense of this habitat. On the other hand, cultivated areas may provide excellent habitat for some grassland birds. Grinnell and Miller (1944) note that "various cultivated crops, but particularly alfalfa, provide the requirements [for Western Meadowlarks] otherwise found in native grasslands."

In Santa Cruz County, grassland is found mainly on the east slope of the Santa Cruz Mountains although patches of northern coastal prairie (Thorne, 1976) are present on the west slope at lower elevations. On the west slope of the Santa Lucias, grassland generally occurs below the live oak-dominated mixed evergreen forest and above the coastal scrub. On the east slope it occurs adjacent to both foothill woodland and chaparral.

Although grassland is used by a large variety of birds, it is the preferred habitat of only a few species. Miller (1951) stated: "Extensive use of grass for ground forage without dependence on it for retreats or nesting partly accounts for the large total avifauna." The White-tailed Kite and the Yellow-billed Magpie are good examples of birds that forage extensively in grassland but use other types of vegetation for shelter or nesting. Of the 55 breeding species of California birds that Miller listed as using grassland at least to some extent, only nine use it as their preferred habitat. Only five of these nine occur in our area as breeding birds—the Burrowing Owl, Horned Lark, Western Meadowlark, Savannah Sparrow, and Grasshopper Sparrow. To these may be added the Lark Sparrow, which often forages and occasionally nests in open grassland.

Although grassland appears superficially to be less varied than woodland or forested areas, it may differ in several important respects from place to place, or even within a limited area. Height, density, and species composition of vegetation, amount and depth of litter, and amount of illumination reaching the ground may vary greatly even in different parts of the same field.

The bird community resident and/or breeding in grassland is limited in numbers, but the ecological relationships among the species are very complex. Cody (1968) studied the passerine bird communities of a large number of different areas representing different types of grassland in the United States and Chile. Wiens (1969) studied very intensively the passerines of a single grassland area in Wisconsin. Although there were some differences in their results (since the two studies were organized so differently), certain consistencies were found.

The grassland species sorted themselves out in groups according to the height and density of the vegetation. Some species, such as the Horned Lark, preferred short, sparse grass; and others, such as the Grasshopper Sparrow, preferred tall, dense grass. Still others were intermediate in their preferences. Where the grass was tall there was a vertical stratification of species, some feeding on or near the ground, others higher up. Differences in foraging behavior were evident. Some species moved through the grass rapidly, with infrequent, short stops; others foraged much more slowly, pausing frequently for lengthy periods. Competition among the grassland species was thus much reduced because of their varied foraging locations and the different ways in which they used the same habitat. Wiens found that the only real competition among the species in his Wisconsin study area was for elevated singing perches. A very significant finding was made by Cody, that where the structure of the grassland was similar in Chile and the United States, the various members of the bird community showed the same differences in habitat preference and use although the Chilean bird and grass species were entirely different than those in the United States.

In addition, there are considerable differences in diet among the grassland birds. The Burrowing Owl is not comparable to the passerines in this regard since it is considerably larger, has a different kind of food-getting apparatus, and takes much larger food items on the average. Of the four true grassland songbirds of the Monterey Bay area, the Western Meadowlark and the Grasshopper Sparrow eat mainly animal matter (about 65 percent; Bryant, 1914; Judd, 1901), whereas the Horned Lark eats an overwhelming proportion of vegetable matter (McAtee, 1905). The Savannah Sparrow is intermediate, eating 46 percent animal and 54 percent vegetable matter (Judd, 1901).

Although the Western Meadowlark and the Grasshopper Sparrow take about the same amount of animal matter, there are pronounced differences in foraging behavior between them. The meadowlark frequently uses its long, sharp bill to probe into the ground in search of food. Coues (1874) noted that freshly thawed ground had been riddled with thousands of holes made by foraging Western Meadowlarks, and La Rivers (1941) reported that in Nevada this species "is by far the ablest avian predator of the Mormon cricket, for it specializes on the eggs of the pest;" these are dug up from below the soil surface. Such probing and digging behavior would be impossible for the Grasshopper Sparrow with its stubby bill, scarcely a third as long as that of the meadowlark. Thus, differences in bill size and shape leading to differences in diet allow further partitioning of the habitat and further decrease in competition among grassland birds.

A recent study indicates that species of sparrows wintering in plains grassland in Arizona occur at different distances from the nearest tree or shrub cover. The method each species uses to avoid predators is determined by the distance of its foraging area from cover. Thus, competition among the various wintering species is lessened by the separation of their foraging grounds (Pulliam and Mills, 1977).

The role of the Western Meadowlark as an important destroyer of insect pests has been discussed by Bryant (1912, 1914) and La Rivers (1941). Bryant (1912) investigated the foraging habits of birds during a very destructive grasshopper outbreak in cultivated fields near Los Banos, Merced County, California. He censused the birds present in the affected area to determine their relative abundance and then examined their stomach contents to determine to what extent they were feeding on grasshoppers. The Western Meadowlark was common in the ravaged fields, ranging from one to five per hectare. The meadowlark stomachs that Bryant examined held an average of 16 grasshoppers each. Since he had found from previous experiments that a meadowlark will digest the contents of a full stomach in two to four hours, he estimated that the average meadowlark in the affected area ate at least 50 grasshoppers a day. On this basis he estimated that the local meadowlarks consumed an average of 24,720 grasshoppers a day, second only to the Red-winged Blackbird, which outnumbered it about five to one. La Rivers (1941) noted that in Nevada a Western Meadowlark may consume as many as 200 eggs of the Mormon cricket in one foraging period and that this species is a major control on the cricket.

The wing/tail ratios of our grassland birds are very high. The Burrowing Owl has a ratio of 2.11; it is tied with the Short-eared Owl for third place among the nine species of owls found in our area. The four passerines range from 1.34 in the Grasshopper Sparrow to 1.65 in the Western Meadowlark. The four true grassland species average 1.47. Compare this to the eight species of mixed evergreen forest (average 1.16) and the ten scrub species (average 0.91). One would expect considerable reduction in tail length in songbirds which spend nearly all their time in grassland. Such birds must move through this relatively dense vegetation when foraging and they frequently escape danger by crouching as low as possible in the sheltering grass. Under such circumstances a long tail would be a considerable liability.

Nesting also presents hazards for birds breeding in grassy areas unsheltered from above. The Burrowing Owl solves the problem by nesting in the deserted burrows of certain mammals. These may be modified or enlarged by the owls. In our area the burrows of the California ground squirrel are used most. Badger burrows are probably used occasionally, as in other areas. Grinnell, Dixon, and Linsdale (1930) excavated an active nesting burrow in Pete's Valley, Lassen County, California. While digging they heard with increasing clarity a sound that closely resembled the buzzing of a rattlesnake. When the nest chamber was reached, it was found that the sound was being made by the six young. They speculated that this sound might deter carnivores such as badgers, coyotes, weasels, and others which might dig up or enter a burrow.

The Horned Lark, nesting in sparsely vegetated or even bare areas, is adept at placing its nest in natural or artificial depressions such as a wheel track or hoofprint; Dawson and Bowles (1909) found a nest placed in the bottom of an unused golf hole. Savannah and Grasshopper sparrows often place the nest under a tussock or overarching clump of grass or they may partially roof it over with long stalks of grass to conceal it from above. The Western Meadowlark routinely roofs its nests completely or nearly so in the same fashion. This roofing, combined with careful placement, makes nests of this species difficult to locate. Yet Dawson and Bowles (1909) noted that Western Meadowlarks nesting in a very closely cropped sheep pasture in Washington carried to their nests long stalks of dry grass to form the protective roof or dome. "As a result one had only to look for grassy knobs on the landscape. By eye alone we located six of these pathetic landmarks in the course of a half-hour's stroll." This is a striking example of how stereotyped behavior, highly adaptive in the great majority of cases, can be most disadvantageous in the wrong circumstances.

The list of birds using grassland is long, but with the exception of the six species discussed previously, these birds occupy this habitat for foraging only, either in the vegetation or, in the case of the kingbird and swallows, in flight above it. The local resident grassland species include the White-tailed Kite, Red-tailed Hawk, American Kestrel, California Quail (occasional nester), Killdeer, Mourning Dove, Barn Owl, Burrowing Owl, Horned Lark, Yellow-billed Magpie, Common Crow, Western Bluebird, Starling, Western Meadowlark, Red-winged Blackbird, Brewer's Blackbird, Brown-headed Cowbird, Savannah Sparrow, and Lark Sparrow. Summer visitants are the Turkey Vulture, Western Kingbird, Violet-green Swallow, Tree Swallow, Rough-winged Swallow, Barn Swallow, Cliff Swallow, and Grasshopper Sparrow.

Freshwater Marshes, Lakes, Ponds, and Rivers

FRESHWATER MARSHES are found along the edges of some of our ponds, lakes, and rivers. Marsh vegetation varies from place to place but includes some or all of the following: narrow-leaved cattail, broad-leaved cattail, wire grass, three-square, California tule, duckweed, sedges, and rushes. In brackish marshes, as at the mouth of the Carmel River, salt marsh species such as salt grass, pickleweed, silverweed, brass buttons, and fleshy jaumea may also occur (Balaguer, 1973).

Marshes associated with ponds and lakes are usually an intermediate stage in a successional series leading from open water to dry land. As deposition of silt continues over a long period of time, the open water gradually disappears and the vegetation changes until eventually the once open water area is filled, becomes dry land, and supports a type of vegetation quite different from what has gone before. Marshy areas along streams, where water moves more rapidly and silt deposition is relatively minor, are not subject to this process.

As Small (1974) notes, there is relatively little competition among the species of freshwater marsh birds because of many interspecific differences in foraging methods, foraging sites, and nature of prey items taken. Some species, such as the Tricolored Blackbird, actually forage some distance from the marsh proper. Great Blue Herons and egrets may seek food in grassland and agricultural areas.

Crespi Pond, Point Pinos, Pacific Grove, showing extensive tule growth in the background. A number of records of birds unusual in our area have been made here. The tules will eventually fill in the entire pond if left undisturbed. (R. Buchsbaum)

Marsh birds are especially interesting because of their mating systems. Of the 291 species of North American passerines which breed north of Mexico, only 14 are regularly promiscuous or polygynous (5 percent or more of the males falling into either or both of these categories). Six of these breed in marshes; two in marshes and either savanna or prairie; three in savanna or prairie; one in scrub; one in scrub and forest edge; and only one in dense forest (Verner and Willson, 1966).

It has been suggested that polygyny results from sexual imbalance within a population. Presumably, if there are appreciably more females than males, some males would attract more than one mate. However, a series of polygynous populations of the Long-billed Marsh Wren in Washington had a sex ratio of 1:1 (Verner, 1964d; Verner and Engelsen, 1970). Balanced sex ratios have been found in populations of several other polygynous species as well.

In order for polygyny to evolve as a mating system, it must be advantageous for both the males and females involved. In other words, the male and females involved in a polygynous breeding unit must produce, on the average, more offspring than if the birds involved had been monogamous. This could come about if a male, already mated, held a good territory and his unmated neighbor held a very poor territory. An unmated female seeking a mate might well do better to mate with the paired male on a good territory than with the single male on poor territory even though the polygynous male would be dividing his time between two nests (Verner, 1964). Under such circumstances, more offspring would be produced by the second female than if she had paired with the single male on his unsuitable territory. Conversely, the total number of offspring sired by the polygynous male would be greater than the number he would have sired with only one mate.

Of course, polygyny can be carried only so far before it becomes disadvantageous as the resources of any territory do have limits. In the Long-billed Marsh Wren, for example, cases of bigamy are common but cases of trigamy are very rare (Verner, 1965; Welter, 1935).

Verner and Willson (1966) noted that two-dimensional habitats such as marshes, savannas, and prairies have more concentrated food resources than would be found in three-dimensional habitats such as forests. Solar energy, ultimately responsible for the production of food, would be concentrated in a relatively narrow vertical zone in the first three habitats but would be spread over a much broader vertical zone in forests. The greater concentration of food in marshes would favor polygyny, since a territory with more than one nesting female would have to support more birds. Further, production in marshes tends to be patchy, with areas of high and low resources in close proximity.

Under these circumstances, a marsh-breeding female seeking a mate has a relatively good chance of encountering successive males with rich and poor territories, respectively, and if the difference between the territories exceeds a certain threshhold (the "polygyny threshhold") she will select the better territory whether or not its owner is already mated (Verner, 1964; Verner and Willson, 1966). It has been suggested that in noncolonial polygynous species such as the Long-billed Marsh Wren, relative abundance of food is the main factor in establishing a "polygyny threshhold" whereas in colonial polygynous species such as the Red-winged Blackbird, the presence or absence of safe nest sites is more important (Wittenberger, 1976). A recent study of polygyny in the Lark Bunting in alfalfa-sparse grass habitat in South Dakota indicated that protection of the nest from solar radiation was the most important factor affecting nesting success there. Males defending territories which provided adequately protected nest sites tended to attract two mates and males with poor territories failed to attract a mate at all (Pleszczynska, 1978).

The breeding habits of some marsh passerines are of considerable interest. The male Long-billed Marsh Wren establishes a territory and builds a number of nests in a restricted area. When a female enters his territory he escorts her to this "breeding center" and she inspects each nest in turn. If she finds none to her liking she leaves to search for another mate. Her decision to stay or to leave is probably influenced primarily by the nature of the male's territory rather than by the nests themselves, unless perhaps they convey some information about the richness of resources on the territory. If the female accepts a nest and stays the male then builds another series of nests elsewhere in his territory and tries to attract another female (Verner, 1965).

The Red-winged and Tricolored blackbirds are apparently closely related species (Mayr and Short, 1970). Yet, a notable study by Orians (1961), mainly of blackbird colonies in the Sacramento Valley, showed great differences in social organization and breeding behavior between them. Male Redwings spend several months establishing their territories, which may average as large as 1300 m^2 in some colonies. Tricolor males establish their territories on the morning of the day on which breeding begins and their territories average a little over 3 m^2. Breeding is much more highly synchronized in Tricolors, with as many as 50,000 to 100,000 nests in a single colony being built within a week's time.

The size of a Red-wing's territory generally determines how much food will be obtained within its limits. Tricolors obtain all of their food outside the limits of their miniscule territories and may fly as far as six kilometers to forage. The foraging area of a single colony may be as large as 78 km^2 (Orians, 1961). Because of the striking differences between the social organizations of the two species and the generally more open breeding habitat used by the Red-wing, there are pronounced interspecific differences in their displays and vocalizations (Orians and Christman, 1968).

Among the nonpasserine marsh birds in our area the Pied-billed Grebe is of particular interest. Its nest consists of a soggy mass of vegetable matter and the eggs are laid in a depression in this mound. When unattended, the parent covers them with wet plant material. At hatching the young are covered with black-and-white striped down, quite unlike the plumage of the parents. Chicks often ride on the back of a parent and when the old bird dives the young go down with it, held in place by the parent's wings. On October 5, 1941, at Carmel River lagoon, Laidlaw Williams noted an adult feeding begging, striped young; at least three young were with the parents (Linsdale, 1942). This is an unusually late record for dependent young still in natal down.

Local resident species which breed and/or forage in freshwater areas are: Pied-billed Grebe, Great Blue Heron, Black-crowned Night Heron, Mallard, Cinnamon Teal, Ruddy Duck, White-tailed Kite, Virginia Rail, Sora, American Coot, Spotted Sandpiper, Belted Kingfisher, Black Phoebe, Long-billed Marsh Wren, Common Yellowthroat, Red-winged Blackbird, Tricolored Blackbird, Brewer's Blackbird, Savannah Sparrow, and Song Sparrow. In summer, the Green Heron is present as a breeder and Tree, Rough-winged, Barn, and Cliff swallows often forage above fresh water.

Estuaries, Beaches, and Marine Rocky Habitats

NORTH OF POINT CONCEPTION the California coast is mostly rocky. There are few significant breaks in the rugged front presented to the Pacific Ocean by the north-south barrier of the Coast Ranges. Among the breaks are the Salinas Valley and Monterey Bay, as well as the enormous complex making up San Francisco Bay and the smaller, but very important, Morro Bay. Between the rocky headlands of the northern and southern limits of Monterey Bay are 36 miles of sand beaches, backed for the most part by large dunes. These otherwise continuous beaches are interrupted by the mouths of the Pajaro and Salinas rivers and the opening to the sea of Elkhorn Slough.

In the last decade much interest has been shown in California's remaining estuarine systems, primarily because of the realization that such areas were being gradually destroyed without much concern for their importance as natural habitats for birds, as nurseries for fishes, and in other ways. This increased interest has greatly advanced our knowledge of the birds of such areas and of the animal and plant communities which support them.

The *California Coastal Plan* (December 1975) states: "Of the original 197,000 acres of marshes, mudflats, bays, lagoons, sloughs and estuaries in California (excluding San Francisco Bay), the natural productivity and open space values of 102,000 (52%) have been destroyed by dredging or filling. Of California's remaining estuaries and wetlands, 62% have been subjected to severe damage and 19% have received moderate damage." In our area, Elkhorn Slough is the most significant coastal wetland because of its size (1,000 hectares of tidal flat and salt marsh) and the variety of estuarine habitats found there.

The Slough itself, and the adjacent areas of the lower Salinas River, have been much modified over the years. Most of the fresh water formerly entering the Slough watershed has been impounded for irrigation or for the creation of stock ponds. Salt evaporation ponds were established on former mudflats and salt marshes, and more recently the natural opening to Monterey Bay was closed off and a more direct one created. These changes are discussed in detail by Gordon (1977).

There are many published works on estuaries, their plants and animals, sedimentation, and hydrography (e.g., Eltringham, 1971; Wolff, 1973; Macdonald, 1977). A particularly useful book on the marine life of estuaries, including birds, is by Green (1968). The natural history of estuarine animals, including many of our local species, is discussed in McGinitie and McGinitie (1968). Unlike the early work of Loomis and Beck on marine birds, there is no important early work on Elkhorn Slough and its birdlife to draw upon, and the first comprehensive account is that by McGinitie (1935). In the first true ecological study of the Slough he described its physical environment in considerable detail and catalogued its marine invertebrate and vertebrate faunas. This study is also important in that it describes the marine life of the Slough before the new entrance to the ocean was made. Birds are covered briefly, emphasizing in a general way the impact of gulls, pelicans, herons, and shorebirds on the invertebrates and fishes. Ricketts and Calvin (1968) provide a lengthy and highly readable

Upper Elkhorn Slough, near the Kirby Park boat access area. Note the broad unspoiled nature of the Slough at this point. In the foreground are freshwater shallows utilized for feeding by Cinnamon Teal and other dabbling ducks, American Coots, Greater Yellowlegs, Long-billed Dowitchers and Common Snipe, among other species. A diked embankment carries the railroad and beyond lies the main channel of the Slough, shown on an ebbing tide. The mud flats provide foraging areas for large numbers of Western and Least Sandpipers, Short-billed Dowitchers, Semipalmated and Black-bellied plovers, Willets, Marbled Godwits and Long-billed Curlews. On the upper right are the extensive *salicornia* salt marshes, used as a high tide roost and feeding ground by many shorebirds and herons. This is the home for a small isolated resident population of the endangered California Clapper Rail. The main channel is frequented by Common and Red-throated loons, Western Grebes, Lesser Scaup, Common Goldeneyes and other species. The Nature Conservancy established the Lillian D. Hohfeld Reserve in this part of the Slough and in the fall of 1979 the Federal Government designated a large portion as a National Estuarine Sanctuary, with a large additional tract to be acquired as a National Wildlife Refuge. (R. Buchsbaum)

discussion of estuarine invertebrates of the Pacific coast, including Elkhorn Slough. Readers needing information on the life histories of our common intertidal animals, especially those important to birds, should consult this work.

Shorebird studies in western North America have expanded greatly in recent years. This interest has in part been generated by concerns over habitat loss. The application of color-banding for following known individual birds and the development of techniques for the identification of invertebrate prey remains have both provided stimulus to these recent studies. For information on a wide range of shorebird topics the reader is referred to Pitelka (1979).

Birds using estuarine habitats face several basic problems. First, most of an estuary is affected by the tidal cycle. On the West Coast we have a mixed, semidiurnal cycle, with (usually) two low tides daily, one considerably lower than the other. Thus, the amount of available feeding space fluctuates with the tide. Tidal cycles provide more feeding space on mudflats in spring than in fall (Recher, 1966). Shorebirds also resort to night feeding in the nonbreeding season (Baker and Baker, 1973). The extent of nocturnal feeding is unknown but humans living or working by estuaries and beaches soon become aware that bird activity is governed more by the status of the tide than by daylight. In recent years birdbanders wishing to catch large numbers of shorebirds have learned to place their mist nets so as to intercept night-flying flocks changing feeding grounds. As important as adequate foraging grounds for shorebirds are secure roosting sites (Cogswell, 1977); islands, sandspits, beaches, and salt pond dikes are all used.

The vast majority of shorebirds using local estuaries and beaches are long distance migrants. They spend only three months on their breeding grounds in the Arctic and sub-Arctic and nine months on migration or in the southern wintering area, where large numbers of shorebirds of many species gather in a limited habitat. According to Recher (1966), northward shorebird migration in spring near Palo Alto, probably much the same as in the Monterey area, begins in late January. It peaks in the last two weeks in April and continues at a lower rate into May. Many immature, nonbreeding shorebirds, usually in immature or winter plumage, stay on and spend the summer on our local estuaries. The southward migration of birds from the northern breeding grounds is usually under way by early July, led by those adults thought to be unsuccessful breeders. Immature birds follow in late August and September and peak fall numbers are reached most often in late October or early November. A decline then occurs, as birds leave for areas to the south, and the winter population stabilizes in December and January.

In the Western Sandpiper, and perhaps some other species, the sexes migrate at different times and apparently winter in different areas, most females moving farther south than most males (Page et al., 1972). In addition to the migrants there are, of course, resident shorebird species which breed locally.

Although estuarine habitats are extremely rich environments for shorebirds, the food on the Arctic and sub-Arctic breeding grounds is even more abundant and more readily available, with 18 to 24 hours of daylight for foraging and no tidal factors to consider. Baker and Baker (1973) stated that food availability and abundance on the far nothern breeding grounds "is the ultimate explanation for the evolution of migratory behavior in these birds."

Only four to at most eight hours of feeding time are available in winter, but Recher (1966) found that the habitats frequented by migrating shorebirds are remarkable for their abundance and constancy of food. This is not true of the northern breeding grounds, where food abundance has a well-marked annual cycle. Further, food is more diverse on the California wintering grounds. Recher believed that the great interspecific variation in such features as size, bill length, and leg length in shorebirds, allowing different species to specialize on different food items, may be a means of lessening competition for food resources in the relatively uniform winter habitat.

Burton (1974) gave a full account of the feeding behavior and food preferences of five species of Eurasian shorebirds, together with a detailed study of the anatomy of the jaws, tongue, and neck in the whole shorebird group. The species in this group may be divided into subgroups according to bill length. First, there are those short-billed species which locate prey visually and *pick it* from the surface of the mudflat or beach. These include the Semipalmated and Black-bellied plovers, Killdeer, and Least Sandpiper. Second, there are longer-billed species which *probe* into the substrate and locate prey by touch. The bill tips of some long-billed species are thought to have unusually well-developed nerve supplies and flexibility. In this group are both species of dowitchers, the Marbled Godwit, Long-billed Curlew, Dunlin, Red Knot, and both species of yellowlegs. In addition, phalaropes by swimming and Black-necked Stilts and yellowlegs by feeding from the water surface, rather than from the bottom, are able to feed in deeper water. Turnstones are further specialized to use prey found under small pebbles and algal fronds. In addition to their long bills and legs their upper mandible and palate have numerous backward-facing projections which help them hold captured food items (Couch, 1966).

In studies of some shorebird populations at Bolinas Lagoon, Marin County, Stenzel et al (1976) analyzed feeding behavior and diet in the Long-billed Curlew and the Willet. They made direct observations of foraging individuals, analyzed remains found in regurgitated pellets, and analyzed substrate cores for measurements of invertebrate abundance. The curlews used their long, curved bills to probe into the burrows of mud crabs, ghost shrimps, and mud shrimps. Willets fed in a much greater variety of habitats and commonly used as many as 30 prey species. They were more evenly distributed among the different coastal habitats than were the other common large shorebirds, and they searched for their prey visually rather than by probing and touch.

These authors also found that the winter decrease in the amount of daylight available for foraging was accompanied by a

Marbled Godwits use their extremely long bills to probe for polychete worms, small marine snails and scallops in Southern California. Their diet in Monterey Bay has not been reported. They frequent a variety of soft substrates, including ocean beaches, mud flats and salt marshes. (R.L. Branson)

decrease in the abundance of some prey species, brought about by winter rains and freshwater runoff. Foraging was less successful and the birds were forced to rely on habitats other than tidal mudflats, and to extend their feeding into the night. The observations at Bolinas Lagoon probably reflect the behavior of these species at Elkhorn Slough.

Curlews commonly feed inland in California although their diet in such grassland areas has not been studied in detail. There are daily flights of wintering flocks from the Elkhorn Slough area to the grassland near Marina.

Hamilton (1975) compared the breeding biology and behavior of the American Avocet and the Black-necked Stilt on a salt pond area in southern San Francisco Bay. Both species fed extensively on brine shrimps and brine flies but competition was avoided because the avocets foraged in shallower water than did the stilts. Intersexual competition was lessened because male stilts fed in deeper water than did females, and male avocets fed more by plunging the head and neck below the surface, females feeding more by pecking at the surface.

In southern California, Marbled Godwits fed mainly on polychete worms, small marine snails, and scallops (Reeder, 1951). Brine flies were taken in salt marshes. The active feeding habits of the Greater Yellowlegs, particularly its erratic running through shallow water, were directed at small fishes, especially mud-dwelling gobies. Dowitchers probed mainly for polychetes.

In general, shorebirds feed on those species which are most numerous and most readily captured (Couch, 1966). On beaches, immature sand crabs are a primary food and reach their peak of abundance in fall and winter when migrant shorebirds use them most. Mud flat food species are dominated by polychete worms. In California fewer gastropod molluscs (snails and their allies) are eaten than their abundance would suggest. Insects and their larvae, especially the shorefly, are important, especially to birds foraging in salt marshes (Reeder, 1951).

Shorebirds take a great toll of marine invertebrates above and between tidemarks and such predation may have influenced the evolution of avoidance behavior in prey species, such as becoming nocturnal or staying in or close to crevices and other refuges (McGinitie and McGinitie, 1968). To test the impact of foraging on prey populations, Schneider (1978) used cages to protect feeding areas from shorebirds. Comparison of protected and unprotected areas showed that shorebirds reduce the relative abundance of the more common prey species. Territoriality among non-breeding shorebirds in coastal California and the pampas of Argentina is described in Myers et al (1979a). Sanderlings wintering on ocean beaches and adjacent mudflats at Bodega Bay, in Sonoma County, establish and vigorously defend territories, the size of which is clearly related to the abundance of their preferred prey, isopods and sand crabs. Color-banding showed that some individual birds maintained their territories for several weeks and returned in successive winters to re-occupy them (Myers *et al* 1979b).

The amount of aggressive behavior shown by shorebirds seems to be correlated with feeding habits and type of foraging site (Recher and Recher, 1969). Long-billed probers show virtually no aggression. Species which locate their prey visually, and with an irregularly distributed food supply, are frequently aggressive on the feeding grounds.

Few studies comparing the same shorebird species on both the breeding and wintering grounds have been done. Baker and Baker (1973) studied six species of shorebirds which breed on Hudson Bay and winter in Florida. They found that in the breeding season there was broad overlap among all six in choice of habitat, in behavior, and in kinds of food eaten. In the winter range there was much less overlap in diet and kinds of habitat used. Of the six species, the Semipalmated Plover showed the least difference between summer and winter feeding behavior. The Dunlin was the most varied and adaptable in general foraging habits.

The size selective feeding habits of the two species of terns which breed at Elkhorn Slough were studied by Baltz *et al* (1979). Forster's Terns foraged over the entire area of the Slough, but primarily over mudflats covered at floodtide, whereas the Caspian Terns foraged over the main channel and to a lesser extent over the shallows. Forster's preyed mainly on juveniles of shiner perch and northern anchovy, with smaller numbers of three other fish species. In contrast, the Caspian Tern fed predominantly on the adults of shiner perch and northern anchovy and took no other species.

Thus far we have been concerned with the shorebirds of the estuarine mudflats. Our coastal wetlands include other habitats, and among the most important are the salt marshes and salt evaporation ponds. The latter are usually found in those parts of the estuary which were formerly mudflats. Finally, most estuaries reach the sea through an area of open beaches. The estuaries of Monterey Bay are no exception.

The extensive network of marshes in Elkhorn Slough and a marsh area on the south side of the mouth of the Salinas River are important and relatively undisturbed salt-marsh areas. They are very important sources of nutrients to the estuary and, together with the Slough itself, they are important nursery areas for marine fishes. They also serve as feeding grounds for estuarine shorebirds where the birds can continue to feed even at high tide, when the mudflats are covered. Many species of shorebirds roost in the salt marshes. In addition, Long-billed Curlews, and Willets in search of lined shore crabs, forage there at low tide.

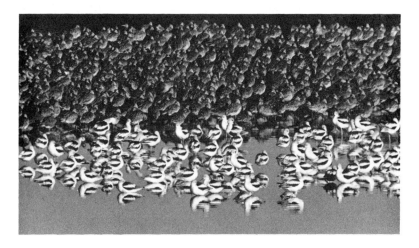

Densely packed Marbled Godwits, above, and American Avocets, below, roosting together at high tide when their feeding grounds become inundated and inaccessible. Such close flocking behavior provides protection from potential predators such as the birds of prey. (F. Lanting)

These marshes are also the only habitat of the endangered California Clapper Rail, first recorded from Elkhorn Slough by Silliman (1915), who reported two nests and stated that the slough was "regularly but sparingly inhabited by these birds." For many years thereafter this rail was not reported there until concern for its status, following its designation as endangered, led to a survey by Varoujean (1973). He found a stable population of about ten pairs nesting in areas where the pickleweed was highest and where nests can escape inundation during high tides. The food of this species in San Francisco Bay included plaited horse mussels, spiders, clams, yellow shore crabs, and the seeds of cord grass (Williams, 1929; Moffitt, 1941), a plant not found at Elkhorn Slough (Gordon, 1977).

Passerines are few in the salt marshes but the Savannah Sparrow is an abundant resident, building its nest in the pickleweed out of reach of spring tides. The birds forage on the mud among the pickleweeds.

Modification of an estuary by the establishment of salt evaporation ponds is not particularly disadvantageous to birds. The areas diked to create the shallow ponds provide good feeding grounds for dense flocks of shorebirds and waterfowl; the dikes themselves often provide ideal breeding grounds for some species and resting areas for gulls, herons, and shorebirds at high tide. The earliest salt ponds in Elkhorn Slough were made in 1916 (Gordon, 1977). In a study of salt ponds in southern San Francisco Bay, Anderson (1970) found that the Northern Pintail, Cinnamon Teal, and Ruddy Duck ate mostly wigeon grass. Brine fly larvae and pupae were the main foods of the shorebirds, including the American Avocet. Northern and Wilson's phalaropes present in late summer fed mainly on water boatmen. Apart from the phalaropes, shorebirds use only those ponds shallow enough to permit wading. Anderson recorded only Eared Grebes and avocets eating large quantities of brine shrimp, although Cogswell (1977) suggests much greater use of this food by phalaropes and other shorebirds.

At Elkhorn Slough the following species show significant use of salt ponds (those marked with an asterisk use them mainly as roosting areas): Eared Grebe, Brown Pelican*, Double-crested Cormorant*, Great Blue Heron, Green-winged Teal, Cinnamon Teal, Northern Shoveler, scaup, Ruddy Duck, Semipalmated Plover, Long-billed Curlew*, Whimbrel*, Willet*, both species of yellowlegs, Least Sandpiper, Dunlin, Short-billed Dowitcher*,

Snowy Egrets, like other wading birds and shorebirds, vigorously defend feeding territories from others of the same species. The size of such territories may be governed in part by prey density. (F. Lanting)

Marbled Godwit, Wilson's Phalarope, and Northern Phalarope.

The abundant food supply and the security provided by the ponds has led several species to breed there. Snowy Plovers, severely depleted on their former ocean beach breeding areas, now nest successfully at salt ponds at Elkhorn Slough and on southern San Francisco Bay. American Avocets and Black-necked Stilts are common breeding birds. The dikes separating ponds have provided the only successful tern nesting sites in recent years in the Monterey Bay region. Both Forster's and Caspian terns have bred there in small colonies. The adults feed mainly in the Slough and adjacent coastal waters rather than on the ponds, which probably contain few fish. Least Terns are seen occasionally, giving rise to the hope that they may breed there.

Groups of birds other than shorebirds make important use of the estuaries. Great Blue Herons, which nested in trees bordering the Slough before the construction of the power plant at Moss Landing, are still frequent visitors. They feed on large estuarine fishes and hunt mice in nearby fields. Great and Snowy egrets eat small mudflat-dwelling fishes (McGinitie and McGinitie, 1968), and at dusk Black-crowned Night Herons glide from the seclusion of daytime roosts in Monterey cypresses to the channels of the Carmel River mouth to fish.

Waterfowl feeding preferences in Elkhorn Slough and the mouth of the Salinas River are not known. On Humboldt Bay eel grass was a very important dietary item; bullrush, spike rush, and barley, found in nearby freshwater marshes and farmlands, were of less importance (Yocum and Keller, 1961). Eel grass beds are thought to have been healthier and more extensive in the past at Elkhorn Slough. It seems clear from fragments quoted by Gordon (1977) that waterfowl were formerly much more common in Elkhorn Slough and on the lower Salinas River, especially before the draining of marshlands for agricultural purposes.

Coastal wetlands and adjacent areas also attract large numbers of raptorial birds. The resident Red-tailed Hawks, their numbers increased by winter visitants from elsewhere, hunt squirrels, smaller rodents, and snakes over many kinds of terrain. White-tailed Kites have staged a remarkable comeback. They are especially conspicuous in the coastal wetlands in autumn as families disperse, hunting rodents in salt marshes and adjacent farmland. Large concentrations gather to feed on the peak vole populations which arise cyclically in the artichoke fields near Castroville and Watsonville, on the borders of the coastal wetlands. Concentrations of over 100 kites have been noted under such favorable feeding conditions.

Golden Eagles are not infrequent visitors to upper Elkhorn Slough. Their appearance is enough to put every local bird to flight, but the eagles are usually more interested in the ground squirrels and rabbits on adjacent slopes. The Bald Eagle and somewhat more numerous Osprey are little more than occasional visitors. Both species probably bred along the lower courses of the major rivers prior to white settlement and there are two early records of Ospreys nesting at Santa Cruz and near Watsonville (Grinnell and Miller, 1944). Marsh Hawks are common in fall and winter, hunting birds and small mammals from the borders of the wetlands. Peregrines are a rare sight these days but were formerly as regular in their appearance as their shorebird and waterfowl prey. Owls are attracted to coastal wetlands, and both Barn and Short-eared owls occur regularly, the latter having bred at least once at the mouth of the Salinas River.

Few good studies of raptor predation on wintering shorebirds have been made. In the winters of 1971-72 and 1972-73, Page and Whiteacre (1975) observed such predation at Bolinas Lagoon. They also analyzed food remains in pellets cast by predators. Of the nine species of predators studied, Merlins were the most successful shorebird hunters but even male American Kestrels killed appreciable numbers of Least Sandpipers. Predation increased in cold weather because shorebirds foraged more intensively and in looser, less compact flocks. The study indicated that isolated individuals were three times more likely to be killed than were flock members. Predation reduced the Dunlin population by 20 percent, Least Sandpipers by 12 percent, Western Sandpipers by 7.5 percent, and Sanderlings by 13.5 percent.

This study supports the suggestion made by Goss-Custard (1970), that predation promotes compact flocking and feeding in shorebirds. Flocking promotes more efficient detection of approaching predators and deters predation. The loud alarm calls sometimes given by wintering shorebirds at the approach of a predator would seem to draw attention to the calling bird. However, such calls alarm nearby birds which fly up and immediately form a flock which the callers can join, thus making them less vulnerable (Owens and Goss-Custard, 1976).

The sand beaches of Monterey Bay are not as rich in shorebirds as are the estuarine habitats. Beaches are less stable and harbor a less varied invertebrate fauna, and this reduces the variety of shorebird species able to forage there. Wave action is another difficulty with which foraging birds must contend. Shorebird use of the beach habitat is divided between species foraging at the water's edge, usually on an ebbing tide, and those which feed mainly in the sand at or above the high water mark. In addition the wrack fauna, those crustaceans and insects inhabiting the band of debris concentrated by wave action at high tide, are important to shorebirds.

The Sanderlings are the most conspicuous birds of our beaches in winter, and the most proficient at exploiting the ever-moving water's edge. By means of very rapid running they follow the edge of a retreating wave, quickly seize their prey, and retreat as the next wave advances. With their sturdy, straight, medium-length bills they probe for sand crabs. At high tide they feed on the sand fleas around tidal debris (Reeder, 1951). In southern California, Sanderlings have been seen to feed on grunion eggs (McGinitie and McGinitie, 1968), and in Washington, sandhoppers and small clams were their most important foods (Couch, 1966).

The Snowy Plover is a common resident of Monterey Area beaches although not as prominent in winter as the Sanderling. Winter flocks tend to use the same limited area of a beach year after year. Their local diet is unknown but in southern California it consists 80 percent of sand crabs, together with beetles, polychete worms, and lined shore crabs (Reeder, 1951).

Snowy Plovers are considered to be threatened because of increasing human disturbance of their ocean beach nesting grounds. Beach nesting locally is confined to those areas, concentrated at the mouths of the Salinas and Pajaro rivers, where there is a broad zone of dry sand above high water. At Pajaro Dunes, on the north side of the Pajaro River mouth, 25 nests were found in 1977 and 31 young were fledged (J. and R. Warriner, personal communication). Successful nesting in the salt pond areas of Elkhorn Slough may help to maintain our local populations.

While often thought of as being confined to ocean beaches, the

Snowy Plover breeds east to Kansas, Oklahoma, and Texas, often in dry lake beds and on alkaline flats. In hot, extremely saline inland habitats they obtain their water from an insect diet and stand in water to lower body temperature when air temperature is high (Purdue, 1975).

Other species which favor dry, sandy areas near and above high water are the Semipalmated Plover, Baird's Sandpiper, Least Sandpiper, and Whimbrel. Willets are common on beaches, feeding on sand crabs. Black-bellied Plovers and Marbled Godwits feed on the lower part of the beach, the former finding their prey visually and picking it from the surface, the latter by probing.

The endangered Californian subspecies of the Least Tern formerly bred north to the old mouth of Elkhorn Slough, on the beach just north of Jetty Road and the present entrance of the Slough into the Bay. The late Laidlaw Williams informed one of us (Baldridge) that there was also a nesting colony on the beach immediately south of the Salinas River mouth where he and the late O.P. Silliman found 21 nests on 16 June 1935. The subsequent history of this colony is unknown. The colony at Elkhorn Slough persisted until about 1950, although a few birds continued to appear in the area each spring for several years thereafter. There was also a colony at the mouth of the Pajaro River from 1939 to 1954 (Pray, 1954). Wilbur (1974) stated that this species prefers undisturbed sandy beaches, close to a coastal lagoon or estuary where its preferred fish food is present. All three former Monterey Bay sites had such characteristics. Although no longer a breeding species in the Monterey Bay area, this bird has established itself in South San Francisco Bay. Beginning about 1966, one or more colonies has nested successfully, if precariously, in suitable man-made habitats. These are usually created by dredge spoil or other fill material. The birds have utilized at least four locations, responding to the impermanent nature of the sites by shifting the colony.

The Least Tern began to disappear from Monterey Bay

Adult Great Blue Heron fishing in a rocky shore tide pool, where several species of blennies may be taken. This versatile wader has also learned to still-hunt fishes from the floating canopy of the forests of giant kelps. (F. Enos)

beaches before human disturbance reached its present level. Perhaps changes in local coastal lagoons, brought about by reduction in fresh water input, or increased pollution from agricultural runoff, were responsible. Those interested in the behavior and breeding biology of this tern should consult Davis (1974) and Massey (1974).

The following species, usually associated with coastal wetlands, have decreased in our area: White Pelican, White-faced Ibis, Bald Eagle, Osprey, Peregrine Falcon, and Least Tern. Clapper Rails probably have declined because of loss of habitat. The White-tailed Kite is the only raptor found in our coastal wetlands known to have definitely increased in California in recent years. Of the shorebirds, Cogswell (1977) states that the Red Knot has increased in California in the past 50 years.

Birds are a conspicuous part of the rocky shore fauna, typified by the flocks of gulls and cormorants perched on rock outcrops, or the flights of Brown Pelicans closely following the shore. This habitat, especially the part exposed at low tide, is used by a variety of bird groups, including both shorebirds and land birds. The environment, exposed to wind and wave action, is more rigorous than that of estuaries and coastal wetlands, and birds of the rocky shore must learn to seek sheltered feeding and roosting sites. They must also learn to avoid wave action when foraging on exposed headlands such as those of the Monterey Peninsula.

Compared with an estuary, the rocky shore has a much greater diversity of invertebrate species. However, this habitat does not attract the great shorebird flocks typical of estuaries. The limiting factor seems to be the diversity of niches for prey species. Many of the rocky shore invertebrates live in crevices or are well hidden in the algal growth so characteristic of this habitat. In addition, many molluscs and barnacles are protected by strong shells and are securely anchored to rocks. Such prey species are largely inaccessible to probers, whereas the latter can feed on invertebrates even when these are buried in the soft mud of estuarine feeding grounds.

One "specialist" inhabiting our rocky shores is the Black Oystercatcher, resident on the Pacific Coast. Its habit of allowing a "midden" of mollusc shells to collect in its nesting area makes its food habits relatively easy to study. At Point Lobos State Reserve its diet consisted mainly of seven species of limpets, with the large owl limpet preferred; also eaten were snails, abalones,

The rocky shore habitat provides a variety of niches for foraging birds. The tidepools in the foreground provide opportunities for the full range of rocky intertidal frequenting shorebirds. Red-breasted Mergansers and Pied-billed Grebes fish in the pools. the guano-covered rocky pinnacles are used by resting cormorants, Brown Pelicans and gulls and a nesting pair of Black Oystercatchers. Beyond lie the rich foraging areas provided by the forests of giant kelps. Surf Scoters, Western and Horned grebes and Elegant Terns feed there. In the sheltered but deeper Bay waters immediately beyond are found Red-necked Grebes, Arctic Loons, Pigeon Guillemots and other species. (R.L. Branson)

chitons, mussels, and crabs (Legg, 1954). In British Columbia, mussels formed most of the diet of both adults and chicks, and limpets were the next most important (Hartwick, 1976). Webster (1941) described in detail the deft way in which the Black Oyster-catcher uses its heavy, chisel-like bill to prey on mussels, limpets, chitons, and barnacles. According to Matthiessen (in Stout, 1967), Black Oystercatchers have calk-like structures on their feet, an adaption for feeding on slippery rock surfaces.

Black Oystercatchers, nowhere common, range from Alaska to Baja California. Unlike other oystercatchers species they are largely resident and do not form large flocks during the non-breeding season. Their black plumage is remarkably cryptic in their algae-covered, rocky intertidal habitat. Numbers may be limited by their choice of nesting site, usually offshore islands, large and small, places which also expose their eggs and young to predation by gulls. Egg clutches are sometimes lost to heavy storm waves. (R.L. Branson)

The Black Turnstone is another shorebird typical of our rocky coast. Although it breeds on the coastal tundra of Alaska the species is rarely entirely absent from the California coast, for many non-breeders remain over the summer. These stocky, short-legged birds with short, slightly upturned bills, are known for their thorough searching technique when foraging. They overturn small pebbles and shells and push aside fronds of seaweeds to reveal the invertebrates hidden beneath. Locally, they have been found to feed on barnacles, periwinkles, limpets, isopods, and amphipods (Glynn, 1965).

Turnstones are most versatile and opportunistic feeders. Some-

Roosting Willets and Black Turnstones at high tide. Both species exhibit winter plumage. Sandspits, dikes and offshore rocks provide safe, undisturbed roosting sites for many species of coast dwelling sea- and shorebirds. (F. Enos)

times they forage among the supine bodies of sleeping California sea lions, perhaps searching for the flies attracted to the herd. Sometimes they go through the scraps left over from a tourist's picnic, or they may dig vigorously into the wrack left by the waves in some sheltered cove. They may also be seen foraging among nesting Brandt's Cormorants at Point Lobos and on the rooftops of buildings on the wharves of Monterey harbor.

Like most of the shorebirds of the rocky shore, their plumage gives turnstones the ability to remain concealed from an observer or a potential predator and when flushed they rise explosively in a welter of wings and a babel of loud cries which might help to confuse a predator at the crucial moment. Sometimes Black Turnstones are accompanied by the closely related Ruddy Turnstone, a much less common species on the Pacific Coast.

Their frequent companions are the Surfbird and the Wandering Tattler. The Surfbird is of a similar stocky build. In small flocks it resorts even more than does the Black Turnstone to rocky islets for foraging, and it keeps closer to the surf. It is often seen about the mussel beds on small, surf-swept rocks, fluttering up as the rock is washed by a wave and settling at once as the water cascades away. Its diet is not known but probably is mainly small crustaceans and molluscs. The Wandering Tattler haunts the same spots as does the Surfbird, but it is usually solitary. Cogswell (1977) notes that in California it is confined to the alga-covered rocky shore, but on Pacific islands it occurs in many kinds of habitat.

Shorebirds of the rocky shoreline must leave their foraging areas at high tide. This period is usually spent sleeping on some secure offshore rock or promontory. Species in this gathering include Black Oystercatcher, Black and Ruddy turnstones, Willet, and Black-bellied Plover. Regurgitated pellets gathered from such roosts can be used to identify prey items consumed. (F. Enos)

Other shore birds of the rocky shore include versatile species such as the Willet, Black-bellied Plover, Whimbrel, Sanderling, and Spotted Sandpiper. Most of the coastal species of gulls occur along the rocky coast but they do most of their foraging elsewhere and rest on the rocks between feeding bouts. The Western Gull does forage in the rocks frequently at low tide, eating sea stars, mussels, crabs, and barnacles.

Large gulls frequently consume sea stars, although the nutritional value to the gulls is questionable. Here a Western Gull is attempting to eat an ochre star. (R.L. Branson)

A surprising number of land birds regularly forage along the shoreline, usually among the rocks. They fall into two groups. First, there are those which forage like shorebirds such as the Black Turnstone. They visit the rocks at low tide, explore the algal cover, or dig into the exposed seaweed wrack. Common Crows, Starlings, and Brewer's Blackbirds commonly do this and

Common Crows (above) and Brewer's Blackbirds (below) are commonly seen foraging the rocky intertidal, as well as the accumulation of wrack on some beaches. Their searching behavior in such environments is similar to that of the Black Turnstone, although their choice of prey is not known (R.L. Branson)

are believed to take both marine invertebrates and the insects of the seaweed fauna.

The second group includes species attracted to the large numbers of flies and other insects associated with beds of decomposing seaweeds stranded by the tide. Black Phoebes, House Sparrows, and especially Yellow-rumped Warblers are prominent members of this group. The phoebe and warbler are winter visitors to the shore and feed on the flying insects of the wrack fauna. The Belted Kingfisher visits the rocky coast in winter and hunts by hovering out over the water or by spotting tide pool fishes from a convenient perch.

Sea cliffs and offshore islets provide foraging areas along the rocky shore and they also provide security to nesting seabirds. These sites are usually safe from such predators as rats, foxes, and raccoons and they become traditional nesting grounds with a long history of use. The headlands of Point Lobos State Reserve and nearby offshore rock stacks have long provided safe nesting areas for Brandt's and Pelagic cormorants, Western Gulls, and Pigeon Guillemots. Such nesting colonies, protected from disturbance but easily observed at close range, are ideal for study.

Bird Island, Point Lobos State Reserve, near Carmel. A large colony of Brandt's Cormorants breeds there (visible as the dark patch, left of center), the size, extent, and success of which varies from year to hear. These fluctuations, according to long-term studies by Point Reyes Bird Observatory biologists on the Farallon Islands, reflect the annual variation in oceanographic conditions and the resulting fish populations. Brown Pelicans formerly nested and still roost in large numbers on this island. (A. Baldridge)

The Brandt's is our most abundant nesting cormorant. At Point Lobos its main nesting site is on Bird Island at the south end of the Reserve but in some years colonies are also found on the north shore at The Pinnacle and on Guillemot Island. Its breeding behavior was described in detail by Williams (1942); the male gathers all the nest material but the nest is built by both members of the pair.

The smaller Pelagic Cormorant nests on narrow ledges on a cliff face. Colonies are small with no more than twenty nests. This species is almost solitary in its foraging, unlike the Brandt's Cormorant, which forages in large groups. The principal predator on the eggs and young of both species is the Western Gull, the only breeding gull of our area, nesting commonly on cliffs and offshore islets along most of the coast. Western Gulls often stand at the edges of a cormorant colony waiting for the opportunity to rob an unguarded nest.

Brandt's Cormorants (left) and smaller Pelagic Cormorants (right) show differences in nesting and feeding habits. Brandt's nests in large closely packed colonies on gently sloping or level sites on offshore rocks, while Pelagics breed in small colonies, usually fewer than 20 pairs, on vertical cliffs, with the nest ledge often overhung. In feeding Brandt's is usually found in large flocks, often hundreds of birds strong, cooperatively driving fish schools in or near kelp beds. Pelagics are usually solitary feeders. (R.L. Branson)

A small breeding colony of the Double-crested Cormorant was discovered by Judson Vandevere in 1961 on an islet off Julia Pfeiffer Burns State Park. This colony is isolated from the nearest breeding groups by many miles and is the only one in our area.

Two species of alcids breed on our rocky coast. Common Murres nest on a few offshore rock stacks along the Big Sur coast south of Carmel. A colony near the Bixby Creek bridge is the most easily observed. The Pigeon Guillemot breeds in small numbers at a number of places, of which Point Lobos State Reserve is the best known. They also breed at the north end of the Bay in low cliffs at Lighthouse Point in Santa Cruz. This species lays its eggs in a natural cavity and is increasing in our area, perhaps because it can use man-made cavities for nesting. Beginning in the late 1960s the birds started nesting under the old canneries in Monterey. This suggests that, as in some hole-nesting species, lack of suitable nest sites, rather than lack of food, limits population expansion. The attractive courtship display of this species has been described in detail by Drent (1965).

Two other species which formerly bred in our area are the Brown Pelican and the Peregrine Falcon. The Brown Pelican was first discovered breeding at Point Lobos by Williams (1927); this was the northernmost breeding colony on the Pacific Coast. The last successful nest was seen in 1959. Its local decline coincided with the decline of the species elsewhere and is thought to have been brought about by increasing DDT residues in the marine environment. Such residues, finding their way into the birds via the prey they consumed, caused them to lay thin-shelled eggs which were either broken by incubating birds, or failed to hatch. Baldridge (1973) has written the history of this colony. The current slow recovery of pelican colonies in southern California, as pesticide levels decrease in the marine environment, gives hope that Brown Pelicans may once again breed in our area.

The Peregrine Falcon nested at Point Lobos until the early 1950s and pairs continued to breed on the Big Sur coast until the mid-1960s. The decline, as for the pelican, was caused by DDT-induced eggshell thinning.

Adult Brown Pelican taking off. This species is an abundant summer and fall visitor to the Bay, with the major roost being at Elkhorn Slough on the dikes of salt ponds, where counts have exceeded 2,000 birds in October. Large numbers also roost on offshore rocks around the Monterey Peninsula. The majority of these birds are thought to be from the Mexican colonies in Baja California. (Ben Lyon, Monterey Peninsula Herald)

Another species inhabiting our local sea cliffs, rather little known locally, is the Black Swift. The first nest known to science, containing a single white egg, as is characteristic of these swifts, was found by A.C. Vrooman (1901) in sea cliffs west of Santa Cruz. Vrooman (1905) later found other nests in the same area. Some of these nest sites were still being used in the late 1960s. Swifts have been seen diving into the cliff face south of Yankee Point, below Point Lobos, presumably to nest sites. In addition, nests have been found in sea caves at the bases of cliffs in our area. The nest of the Black Swift must be located in a very moist site, a requirement nearly unique among North American breeding birds. Coastal sites are close to surf and are saturated with moisture. Inland nests are located near or behind waterfalls in an equally moist atmosphere. The size of the coastal population is difficult to estimate because the birds are only seen feeding along the shore infrequently. Instead they hunt for insect prey above the high ridges inland from the coast. The nest site may be unvisited for several hours at a time. Black Swifts were seen flying over the Hastings Reservation on July 7, 1956, and August 31, 1954. White-throated Swifts are also resident along the rocky coast.

Nestling Black Swift in its moisture saturated, algae made nest in a sea cave in Santa Cruz county. The single young bird does not leave the nest until early September when the birds depart for virtually unknown wintering grounds in South America. (R.L. Branson)

Seabirds: Inshore and Pelagic

Monterey Bay has long been famous for the great numbers and variety of its seabirds, and Monterey is a favorite embarkation point for offshore birding trips. The earlier studies of the marine birds of this area made by Loomis (1895, 1896, 1900a, 1900b) and Beck (1910) were mainly descriptive and emphasized what kinds of birds were present at different times of the year. The oceanographic studies which explained the seasonal and spatial distribution of our seabirds did not come until later. Ainley (1976) analyzed the occurrence and distribution of 28 marine bird species throughout California coastal waters, in relation to ocean temperature, salinity, and productivity. For a detailed discussion of this topic the reader is referred to that paper. Recently, Stallcup (1976) presented useful information on the seasonal status, numbers, and field identification of the pelagic birds of the Bay. An account of all California water birds both freshwater and marine, has been compiled by Cogswell (1977). Detailed information on the distribution and biology of many of our marine birds may be found in Palmer (1962, 1976).

The topography of the Bay includes a shoreline of shale at the northern end, followed by many miles of sandy beaches backed by a system of large sand dunes. The southern end consists of the granite headlands of the Monterey Peninsula. The shoreline is further indented where the Pajaro and Salinas rivers and Elkhorn Slough enter the Bay. Kelp beds fringe the shoreline wherever the bottom is rocky but are absent where it is composed of mud or sand. Beyond the kelp beds the sea floor levels off at a depth of 40 m, gradually sloping away to the edge of the very narrow continental shelf, which is bisected by the Monterey Submarine Canyon, 1800 m deep. Enclosed as it is on three sides, the Bay is well protected much of the time and part of it provides shelter for seabirds no matter from which direction the wind comes.

The rich marine environment of the Bay is created by a combination of oceanographic conditions and topographic features.

Youngbluth (1976) describes three overlapping oceanographic seasons, governed largely by prevailing winds, as follows.

First, the **Upwelling Period.** From March to August, the prevailing northerly winds and the earth's rotation cause the southerly flowing waters of the California Current, within 100 km of the shore, to move away from the coast. They are replaced by cooler, more saline, nutrient-rich water, upwelling from deeper regions. These waters provide favorable conditions for the production of planktonic microorganisms.

Second, the **Oceanic Period.** The northerly winds subside from September through November, and surface water temperatures increase to their maximum of 15°C. This warming occurs as upwelling ends and tongues of warmer, offshore oceanic waters invade. Oceanic species of plankton and fishes reach the coast in this period.

Third, the **Davidson Current Period.** From December through February, when southerly winds prevail, a northward-flowing inshore current develops. This period has less effect on the bird life of the Bay than the first two.

The reader interested in a more detailed account of the annual hydrographic cycle in the Bay is referred to Bolin and Abbott (1963).

The enriched waters of the Bay provide a favorable environment for the first stage in the marine food chain, the growth and multiplication of planktonic organisms, most of them one-celled and capable of photosynthesis ("phytoplankton"). These, in turn, are consumed by larger, multicellular planktonic organisms ("zooplankton") and by small, schooling filter-feeding fishes. Areas of upwelling are among the most productive of marine environments; upwelling is associated with the California Current system from mid-Baja California to Oregon. Within this region, some of the highest concentrations of zooplankton are in the waters in and adjacent to Monterey Bay

(Thrailkill, 1963) and form the basis of the food chain which supports seabirds, large predatory fishes, and marine mammals.

The conspicuous and extensive kelp beds, found wherever the sea bottom is hard, are dominated by the giant kelp and the bull kelp. There can be little doubt that kelp forests are among the most productive systems in the world (Pearse and Gerard, 1977). These kelp beds damp wave action, thus creating areas of calm, protected waters much frequented by seabirds. They also shelter a great abundance and variety of fishes and invertebrates (Quast, 1971a, 1971b; Limbaugh, 1955). The invertebrates are fed upon by larger fishes in turn become prey to diving birds and marine mammals.

The seabirds of Monterey Bay may be divided into two general groups. Many species are found landward of the 50 m depth line; they are properly termed *inshore* or *coastal* species. Among the most typical are the loons, the cormorants, and most terns. *Pelagic* species are those which spend most of their lives beyond the edge of the continental shelf and which usually resort to oceanic islands to breed. Albatrosses, shearwaters, and storm-petrels are the most obviously pelagic groups.

Comon Loons (illustrated) are solitary inshore feeders on sand dabs, herring, surf-perch, rockfish and sculpins (Cogswell, 1977). In contrast the more abundant Arctic Loon feeds in flocks, sometimes of large size, in deeper waters where its diet is greatly supplemented by market squid and crabs (Morejohn, et al 1978). (R.L. Branson)

Habitats are not as numerous or as sharply defined in the marine environment as they are on land. However, seabirds may be assigned to various food niches, depending on their foraging methods and their diets. Ashmole (1971) has described a number of types of foraging used by seabirds. There are those species which swim below the surface, using only the feet for locomotion (cormorants, loons, grebes); others "fly" under water, using both wings and feet for propulsion (Sooty Shearwaters; all alcids); some plunge-dive from the air and reach their prey while moving at relatively high speed (Brown Pelicans, most terns, some gulls; Sooty Shearwaters may plunge-dive and then "fly" under water). Others feed while settled on the water surface, where they may seize individual prey items, scavenge, or surface-filter small animals (Black-footed Albatross, Northern Fulmar, Pink-footed Shearwater). "Hydroplaning," a variation on this method, is apparently used by New Zealand Shearwaters.

Black-footed Albatross flock scavenging alongside a fishing boat. While there are records for all months of the year, the peak numbers occur from May to August. It consumes a wide variety of prey species and is therefore considered to be a generalist. Its breeding grounds lie in the west-central Pacific, especially in the Hawaiian Islands National Wildlife Refuge. (R.L. Branson).

First year Sabine's Gull. The small delicate bill and rather long wings enable this species to capture its plankton prey while on the wing. It is a spring and fall migrant, usually in small flocks and visits offshore waters while in transit between its tundra breeding grounds and its winter range in cold waters off the coast of Peru (R.L. Branson)

Some species, while flying, capture prey at the surface (terns; Black, Ashy, and Fork-tailed storm-petrels; gulls). Some of these birds, especially the storm-petrels and some gulls, will also "patter" with their feet against the water surface to help keep their bodies at a precise height above the surface. "Piracy" or aerial pursuit is used by one bird to rob another of its food. The best known species using this technique are Parasitic and Pomarine jaegers and the Skua, which parasitize gulls, terns, and shearwaters. Some gulls, especially the Heermann's Gull, also obtain food in this manner. The Brown Pelican is a favorite victim of the Heermann's Gull.

Phillips (in Simmons, 1972) recognized three types of seabird plumage associated with feeding method. First, there is the "swimmer," in which white is confined to the plumage below the waterline, the upper parts being dark, as in loons and alcids. This is an adaptation found primarily in seabirds which pursue fish underwater and spend much time swimming at the surface. Such plumage camouflages the bird from its prey below and also protects the bird from underwater predators approaching from

Adult Parasitic Jaeger (pale phase). A spring and fall migrant through the area with occasional overwintering taking place here. This species is common close to shore, where it pursues coastal terns which tend to be concentrated over kelp beds and river mouths. Its larger congener, the Pomarine Jaeger, is more abundant offshore, pursuing larger gulls and shearwaters. Both species secure much, although not all, of their food by aerial piracy. (R.L. Branson)

below. Second, there is the "plunge-diver" plumage, in which the white extends to the head, breast, and underwings, and often includes the leading edge of the wing. This type of plumage is found in many gulls and terns. Third, the "all white" plumage is characteristic of some gulls. This is found in social feeders, those forming or joining feeding groups.

Lack (1968) pointed out that among seabirds, offshore feeders such as murres and Cassin's Auklets have larger colonies than inshore feeders such as cormorants and Pigeon Guillemots. Large colony size may aid offshore feeders in locating foraging sites in the open ocean (Ward and Zahavi, 1973). If a stream of birds were continuously leaving for, and returning from, offshore feeding grounds, an individual bird, setting out from the colony to forage, could follow the stream of birds to the

Cassin's Auklet is a krill feeder and in central California its diet is almost entirely euphausiid crustaceans. In calm conditions these invertebrates sometimes form huge pink swarms in surface waters over deep waters along the edge of the Monterey Submarine Canyon. In such favorable feeding conditions many hundreds of Cassin's Auklets will gather to feed, in addition to shearwaters, phalaropes, and gulls. (A. Baldridge)

feeding site. An inshore feeder need merely fly up or down the coastline to encounter other feeders, even though they are few in number.

The seemingly uncanny ability of pelagic birds, ranging over open ocean, to locate food sources rapidly is well illustrated by an anecdote recounted by the late Robert Cushman Murphy (1925). The peerless collector of marine birds, Rollo H. Beck, chartered a boat to take him off the coast of Peru. The captain and crew had had considerable experience in these waters. One morning Beck requested that a boat be lowered so that he could collect, although not a single bird was in sight. The puzzled captain lowered a boat and a crew member rowed Beck some two miles out. Beck threw out meat scraps and clots of grease as the boat progressed. On return, the course was cluttered with seabirds. Beck returned with specimens of many kinds, all of them unfamiliar to the experienced sailors. One may guess that one or two birds sighted the food and other birds followed them, in turn attracting other birds until a feeding group was formed.

One difficulty faced by seabirds is the lack of water for drinking. Ornithologists had made a number of observations of seabirds drinking seawater, but it was not known how they were able to tolerate it. The mystery was solved by the physiologist Knut Schmidt-Nielsen (Schmidt-Nielsen and Fange, 1958; Schmidt-Nielsen et al, 1958; Schmidt-Nielsen and Sladen, 1958).

It had been known for many years that all birds possessed paired glands in the head, the so-called nasal glands, and that they were best developed in seabirds; their function was unknown. Schmidt-Nielsen and his co-workers noted that when captive gulls were fed salt water, a clear, colorless fluid began to drip from the beak within a short time. This fluid was extremely salty and contained a very high concentration of sodium chloride ("table salt"), far higher than is found in seawater. Microscopic examination of the nasal glands and their functioning in gulls and other marine birds showed that they acted as filters to remove sodium and other ions from the blood following the drinking and assimilation of seawater. The filtrate passes through ducts from the gland to the nostrils and, in most species, flows from the nostrils down the beak. It is this filtering process that enables seabirds to drink the water where they live.

Schmidt-Nielsen coined the term "salt glands" for the nasal glands in those species in which they function to remove sodium and other ions from the blood after salt water ingestion. Shoemaker (1972) lists 13 orders of birds containing 21 families in which functional salt glands have been found. They do not occur in most landbirds, including the songbirds.

A comprehensive review of the feeding habits and trophic relationships of seabirds from California to the Bering Sea, incorporating published and unpublished sources, is provided by Ainley and Sanger (1979). The authors compare the diets of each seabird species throughout its North Pacific range.

Information on the food habits of the seabirds of the Bay has, until recently been very limited. Baltz and Morejohn (1977) analyzed the stomach contents of 17 species of Bay seabirds, exclusive of sea ducks. They also analyzed statistically the amount of dietary diversity of each species and the amount of dietary overlap between pairs of species. Two food items were found to be of special importance—the market squid and the northern anchovy. More important to us than the details of individual diets are the degree of competition for food between and among various species and what factors tend to mitigate this competition.

As these authors point out, the group of species which they studied includes divers, plungers, surface feeders, and scavengers. Therefore, even when the same food item is being used by several species, they may be using different segments of the prey population. They found that the Sooty and Short-tailed (Slender-billed) shearwaters had high food niche overlap, but the Sooty reaches peak abundance in summer and the Short-tailed in January and February, when all but a few Sooties have disappeared. Thus competition between them is avoided by different seasonal occurrence. The Common Murre and the Rhinoceros Auklet are about the same size, occupy the same habitat, get their food in the same way, and use at least six of the same prey species. However, 70 percent of the auklet's diet is market squid, compared to 19 percent for the murre. Here, competition is lessened by differential use of prey items.

Six species of gulls were studied, and food niche overlap was high among five. The Bonaparte's Gull, the smallest of the six, was quite distinct from the others in its preference for small prey items, especially small invertebrates (93 percent of the diet). The other species are all opportunistic feeders, taking many kinds of food and doing considerable scavenging. Many gulls have learned to follow ships and feed on discarded trash fish and offal, and this undoubtedly helps to alleviate competition among them.

The importance of the market squid to the marine birds of the Bay was described in a second study by Morejohn et al (1978). In

Rhinoceros Auklet in winter plumage. This species is the most abundant bird in the offshore waters of the Bay during the winter months. While complete censuses of the scattered flocks are difficult to make, the population is thought to exceed 10,000. Its winter diet is dominated by market squid, supplemented by northern anchovies and other fishes. It is one of the predominant species making up the large multi-species feeding aggregations of seabirds. Although it breeds as near as the Farallon Islands off San Francisco, the main colonies extend from Washington north to Alaska. The origin of the Bay birds is presently unknown. (R.L. Branson)

this case stomach contents of 513 birds of 28 species were examined. An index of the relative importance of prey species was given and food webs showing the relationships of different bird predators to the primary prey species, squid, anchovy, and krill were illustrated. To gain some understanding of the relative impact of seabirds on commercial fisheries, and vice versa, additional experiments were undertaken. These involved the feeding of anchovy and squid to captive Sooty Shearwaters, to produce information on the feeding energetics of the Bay's most abundant seabird. From this the authors estimated that the Sooty Shearwater population in the Bay, estimated to range from 4000 to 1 million birds annually consumes from 36 to 9000 metric tons of squid and from 18 to 4,400 metric tons of anchovies.

Though little information is available on the diets of the sea ducks of the Bay and the amount of food niche overlap among them, work on sea ducks elsewhere suggests interspecific differences in habitat and food. Studies on New Hampshire sea ducks by Stott and Olson (1973) showed that scoters preferred the waters off sandy beaches and fed almost entirely on bivalve molluscs, especially clams. Bufflehead and Common Goldeneyes occurred both in estuaries and along the open coast, but there were important dietary differences between them. Studies on sea ducks of the Bay, similar to those of Baltz and Morejohn (1977) on other groups, are needed to give information on how resources are partitioned among the various species.

Storm-petrels and both the Northern and Red phalaropes feed on zooplankton and some birds, especially the storm-petrels, take advantage of the nightly migration from deep to

Gulls secure their food from a variety of marine habitats, ranging from beaches, mudflats, and rocky intertidal to the offshore waters of the open ocean. Between feeding forays during the day they gather to form "clubs" where they rest, preen, and bathe. California Gulls predominate in the foreground while the more cryptic Heermann's Gulls pack closely together behind. (R.L. Branson)

Sooty Shearwaters eclipse by their abundance all other species of marine birds occurring in the Bay and nearby waters. Their numbers are at their peak from May through August, although they are present in smaller numbers during the remainder of the year. When attracted close to shore in their thousands by spawning market squid they provide one of the great avian spectacles of the North Pacific. (R.L. Branson)

Surf Scoters are abundant winter visitors to sheltered inshore waters, where they are bottom feeders. On warm days in late winter a swimming group will often erupt in a flurry of courtship as several males pursue a female. (R.L. Branson)

Red Phalarope in breeding plumage. An abundant fall migrant along shore as well over offshore waters. In years of unusual abundance the birds overwinter here too. The species is much more unpredictable in its spring occurrence, normally taking an offshore route to the north. (R.L. Branson)

surface waters of the community of fishes and invertebrates known as the "deep scattering layer." These birds feed at night, probably locating their prey by means of its luminescence and perhaps by using a highly developed sense of smell (Grubb, 1972).

Feeding groups composed of several species of seabirds are not uncommon, attracted to a particular area by the appearance of schooling fishes or by the presence of a fishing boat discarding unwanted fishes and offal. One of the commonest feeding associations is that involving anchovy schools in winter. On a calm day these will appear at the surface and gulls of four or more species will converge on the area of activity from as far as 4 km away. The direct flight of the gulls attracts other species, iuncluding Brandt's Cormorants, Arctic Loons, Common Murres, and Rhinoceros Auklets. They take wing and appear to follow the converging gulls. Within five minutes, 500 birds may be involved in pursuing the fish school, with birds dipping, plunging, and pursuit diving. In summer and fall, schools of bonito, a

Schooling northern anchovies attracted this large mixed flock of seabirds made up of Brown Pelicans, Brandt's Cormorants, Heermann's and Western gulls. (F. Lanting)

Pink-footed Shearwaters are the largest of the commonly occurring shear-waters in the Bay. In normal years they appear in the spring, remain through the summer and peak in numbers in the fall. There are a few winter records. Anchovies and other fish make up the major part of their diet followed by market squid (Morejohn, et al 1978). This species will scavenge from fishing boats. (R.L. Branson)

An immature Western Gull follows a feeding sea otter in search of scraps ...

member of the tuna family, may appear in oceanic waters off the Bay. They vigorously pursue schools of smaller fish which, in their efforts to escape, take to the air in a series of low jumps. Here they are eagerly seized by attendant gulls, terns, and jaegers. Flocking behavior under such circumstances conveys information to other individuals about the distance and direction of a food source (Ward and Zahavi, 1973).

Feeding associations between seabirds and marine mammals are not unusual. Groups of feeding sea lions, sometimes only a single feeding individual, may attract gulls and shearwaters. Feeding killer whales are normally attended by gulls, and Western Gulls are often seen close to feeding sea otters, gleaning dropped morsels from the water and sometimes snatching the food item from the otter.

It is very difficult to estimate the impact of seabirds on their prey species, and such studies are rare. Wiens and Scott (1975) estimated that the Oregon populations of the Sooty Shearwater, Leach's Storm-petrel, Brandt's Cormorant, and Common Murre

... while here, an adult consumes a large morsel. Gull/otter interactions are the most frequently observed of marine bird and mammal encounters. (From *The California Sea Otter: Saved or Doomed* by John Woolfenden. Photos by J.A. Mattison, Jr.)

consume 62,500 metric tons annually. Anchovies account for 43 percent of the total (with 86 percent of these fish taken by the shearwater). These four species may consume as much as 22 percent of the annual production of the fishes on which they prey.

Although it is rarely possible to get accurate estimates of total breeding populations of birds, seabirds are an exception. Their colonial habits and often restricted breeding sites lend themselves to accurate censusing. Ainley and Whitt (1973) estimated the total numbers of breeding *pairs* of marine birds from the Oregon border to San Francisco County (including the Farallon Islands). The five most abundant species, with total nesting pairs in parentheses, were: Common Murre (58,120); Cassin's Auklet (53,775); Brandt's Cormorant (15,937); Western Gull (12,026); and Leach's Storm-petrel (8,350).

Mortality among seabirds is often high, particularly during winter months. In the Monterey Bay area there are in some winters massive die-offs of Northern Fulmars and Black-legged Kittiwakes; these appear to correlate with oceanographic con-

Northern Fulmar (light phase). A winter visitor to the Bay with considerable fluctuation in abundance from year to year. Its visits are often accompanied by a noticeable mortality. Some remain during the summer. Its feeding habits include scavenging the carcasses of dead seabirds, including other Northern Fulmars, as well as those of marine mammals. (R.L. Branson)

ditions (D.G. Ainley, personal communication). At the same time, large numbers of dead fish-eating, diving birds, such as Western Grebes and Brandt's and Pelagic cormorants, are found. It is not known whether such deaths are caused by high pesticide levels, food shortage, or a combination of the two. Oil contamination kills many Common Murres and Western Grebes, as anyone who walks the Bay beaches in winter will discover. It is interesting to note that natural oil seeps were recorded killing murres and Rhinoceros Auklets in the Bay in 1895 (Loomis, 1896).

The pesticide burden carried by Bay seabirds has been well established (Risebrough et al, 1967). The Brown Pelican disappeared as a breeding species from Point Lobos State Reserve coincident with the rise in DDT levels and the pelican's decline in other areas (Baldridge, 1973). A new pollutant has recently been discovered by Baltz and Morejohn (1976). Particles of plastic were found in many of the stomach contents analyzed by them. Other causes of mortality have been observed locally.

Severely oiled Common Murres. We may witness an increase in such incidents as offshore oil fields are exploited and the resulting products are moved by undersea pipelines and tankers. (Monterey Peninsula Herald)

On several occasions large numbers of Sooty Shearwaters, apparently confused when feeding inshore at night in dense fog, were fatally attracted to street lighting in Santa Cruz (V.L. Yadon, personal communication). During spring migration unusually strong northwesterly winds have caused substantial mortality in both Red and Northern phalaropes. Predation by predatory fishes and marine mammals has been reported elsewhere but not yet documented for the Bay. Red tides, caused by high concentrations of certain toxin-producing micro-organisms known as dinoflagellates, have caused heavy kills of fish and fish-eating seabirds elsewhere on the Pacific coast, but thus far none has been noted in the Monterey Bay area. The impact of fishery-associated mortality on Monterey Bay seabirds is unknown at present. Should the fishing effort be intensified and involve increased use of gill-nets and long-lines, then an increased toll of marine birds can be expected. For a discussion of the serious problem in the North Pacific and elsewhere, the reader is referred to King et al (1979).

The devastating effects of the periodic warming of the normally cold waters of the Peru (or Humboldt) Current on seabirds has been described by Murphy (1936) and others; mass starvation occurs because of the great decrease in the productivity of ocean waters. Similar, although less pronounced, warming occurs along the California coast but the effects of this on California's marine bird populations have just begun to be investigated. Until the monitoring of seabird breeding success on the Farallon Islands was initiated by the Point Reyes Bird Observatory, no long-term studies were available to evaluate the effects on seabirds of temperature changes in the California Current. It appears at present that breeding success of the Brandt's and Pelagic cormorants and of the Cassin's Auklet have been adversely affected on the Farallons.

The periodic intrusion of warmer water from the south into Monterey Bay has brought with it notable changes in the fish, invertebrate, and sea turtle faunas (Glynn, 1961; Radovich, 1961). It is during these periods of warmer water that pelagic bird species, normally found in Mexican waters, may be looked for in Monterey Bay. These include the Magnificent Frigate-bird, Manx Shearwater, Least Storm-petrel, and Craveri's and Xántus' murrelets. Varoujean and Campagno (1973) correlated the appearance of three Magnificent Frigate-birds in the Bay in September 1971 with water temperatures which were 3°C higher than normal.

Changes in abundance are hard to establish with certainty, but it appears that the following species are markedly less common in the Bay than they once were (Loomis, 1895): Short-tailed Albatross, Short-tailed Shearwater, Manx Shearwater, Royal Tern, Marbled Murrelet, Ancient Murrelet, Parakeet Auklet, and Tufted Puffin. The albatross is known to have barely escaped extermination by Japanese plume hunters on its western Pacific breeding islands. It was an inshore species and was known to frequent the edges of the kelp beds around the Monterey Peninsula shoreline and to follow the local Chinese fishing boats. Loomis (1896) mentioned seeing a dozen or more off Point Pinos in the course of an hour.

The Tufted Puffin's decline is thought to be related to that of the Pacific sardine (Ainley and Lewis, 1974). Loomis (1896) described the puffin as "quite common" in Monterey Bay and he alluded to possible breeding on an islet in Carmel Bay. The disappearance of the Pacific coast subspecies of the Manx Shearwater from the Bay area may have been linked also to the decline of the sardine. Loomis recorded 2,000 Manx Shearwaters moving south off Point Pinos on 11 January 1895 and he clearly indicates their abundance in the Bay in other years. They have often gone unrecorded in recent years and even when seen, their numbers are miniscule compared with their former abundance. Their present distribution, off northwestern Baja California, coincides with that of the Pacific sardine. It may be that the decline of the fish was followed by the decline of the shearwater.

For the other species previously mentioned, we may only speculate. The Ancient Murrelet, the first Californian specimen of which came from the Bay (Stejneger, 1886), was common enough near the kelp beds for Loomis (1895) to collect 102 specimens. Its abundance there today is much reduced. It has also declined greatly as a breeding species in British Columbia (Nelson and Myres, 1976). This has been attributed either to biocides having reduced its preferred zooplankton food or to the presence of warm waters between 1957 and 1971. The late Laidlaw Williams (personal communication) indicated that this species was much more common on Monterey Bay in the 1950s than later.

On the "plus" side, it is difficult to point with certainty to any species of seabird that is more common now than in the time of

Elegant Terns are common in the Bay in summer and fall, following their post-breeding northward dispersal from their island rookeries in the Gulf of California. The reasons for the increase in abundance are unknown. They appear to have replaced the now rare Royal Tern in the Bay and greatly outnumber it in southern California. Protection of their major nesting sites from commercial egging may have been a factor. (R.L. Branson)

Loomis and Beck. The only species which seems definitely to be more numerous at present is the Elegant Tern (Small, 1974). Ashy and Black storm-petrels may be more numerous at present; Loomis and Beck do not appear to have observed them in the large numbers seen today. Horned Puffins, long considered very rare in California, have showed an increased frequency of occurrence in recent years (Hoffman et al, 1975). The reason for this is unclear.

The great increase in the numbers of birders in the last decade, and the publication of more sophisticated criteria for the identification of difficult species, has added to our knowledge of such rarities as the Yellow-billed Loon (Remsen and Binford, 1975) and the Thick-billed Murre (Yadon, 1970a) in the Bay area.

Both were unrecorded in California until recent years, but careful field work has shown both to be annual visitors in small numbers to the Bay.

A final indication of the seabird riches of the area and the continuing excitement of new discoveries may be found in the following species, which have been recorded nowhere else in the United States: Gal-apagos Storm-Petrel (Yadon, 1970b) and Streaked Shearwater (Morejohn, 1978), both wanderers from other parts of the Pacific. In addition, in August 1974 the discovery of the first North American nest and the only known downy chick of the Marbled Murrelet in Big Basin Redwoods State Park, Santa Cruz County, 10 km due east of the coast, concluded a search which had intrigued ornithologists for 185 years (Binford et al, 1975). The nest was located 45 m above ground on a horizontal limb of a Douglas fir. This remarkable site, presumably typical for the species, explains the long delay in its discovery.

Despite the richness of the Bay's seabird fauna, only 9 species are known to breed on or near the coasts of Santa Cruz and Monterey counties. These are the Double-crested, Brandt's, and Pelagic cormorants, the Western Gull, the Forster's and Caspian Terns, the Common Murre, the Pigeon Guillemot, and the Marbled Murrelet. In addition, the Brown Pelican formerly bred at Point Lobos State Reserve and may perhaps resume this status in the future. The remainder of our seabirds are visitors from various parts of both the Northern and Southern hemispheres.

12

HISTORY OF MONTEREY BAY ORNITHOLOGY

In THE LATTER PART of the 18th century it was fashionable for certain European countries, especially France and England, to send out ships on voyages of discovery, often hopefully called "voyages around the world." Almost always, these exploring expeditions carried one or more "naturalists," whose duty it was to collect geological samples, specimens of plants and animals, and anything else that might be of scientific value. Sometimes the ship's surgeon doubled as naturalist. These collections were brought back to Europe and turned over to specialists for critical examination. Often the plant and animal specimens proved to be new to science and furnished the material for the formal descriptions of new species.

Since Monterey was one of the few adequate settled harbors on the Pacific coast, many of these exploring parties put in there to reprovision. The crews' naturalists often took advantage of such opportunities to go ashore and make collections. Just as Monterey was the most important settlement in the early political history of California, so it was also the most important settlement in the early history of that state's ornithology.

J. F. G. de La Pérouse commanded the French frigates *Boussole* and *Astrolabe* on a "voyage around the world" that started in 1785 and ended with the tragic disappearance of both ships and their crews near the New Hebrides in 1788. This ill-starred flotilla put in to Monterey from September 14 to 24, 1786, and its naturalists collected a number of specimens in the immediate area. The account of La Pérouse's voyage was

published in 1797 (Milet-Mureau, 1797) and an English edition
was published in 1798 (Milet-Mureau, 1798). The magnificent
Atlas of plates accompanying the text, examined by us in the
Bancroft Library of the University of California, Berkeley, contains two plates of California birds based on account specimens
collected at Monterey. One, captioned "Perdrix, mâle et femele,
de la Californie," shows a male and female California Quail. The
other, captioned "Promerops de la Californie septentrionale,"
portrays a California Thrasher. Interestingly, the thrasher was
referred to a genus of honeyeater (Meliphagidae) which is found
only in southern Africa.

California Quail, male and female, from a plate in an English edition (London,
1798) of La Pérouse's *Voyage Around the World*. This is one of the earliest
published illustrations of Californian birds.

The next explorer to contribute to California ornithology was Captain George Vancouver, commanding the British ship *Discovery,* which put in at Monterey from November 26, 1792, to January 14, 1793. Archibald Menzies, naturalist for this expedition, collected a number of birds during this stay. He undoubtedly obtained the specimens on which were based the formal descriptions of the California Condor and the California Quail by Shaw and Nodder (1797). The plates illustrating them in Shaw and Nodder's work, published in 1797, along with the two plates in the *Atlas* of La Pérouse's voyage, appearing in the same year, are the earliest published illustrations of California birds.

In 1827 Monterey was visited twice by H.M.S. *Blossom,* commanded by Frederick William Beechey, January 1 to 5 and October 29 to November 17. Beechey had with him several naturalists, but Surgeon Alexander Collie was by far the most energetic collector of birds among them. His specimens were later turned over to the eminent zoologist N.A. Vigors, who was born in Ireland but spent most of his life in London. Vigors (1829, 1839) described two new species from Collie's Monterey material, the Black Turnstone and the Pigmy Nuthatch. He also described as new species several other birds from this material; these are now considered subspecies of birds described by others prior to Vigors' publications.

Thomas Nuttall, an eminent botanist and ornithologist, was the next ornithologically important visitor to Monterey. Although born in England, Nuttall lived and worked in the United States from 1808 until 1842. From 1825 to 1834 he was the curator of the botanical gardens of Harvard University. Nuttall visited the coast of California from March to May, 1836, stopping briefly at Monterey and other coastal settlements. He was the "Professor N---" mentioned by Richard Henry Dana, Jr., in *Two Years before the Mast,* the passenger who boarded Dana's ship, the *Alert,* in San Diego for passage to Boston. Nuttall's major contribution to American ornithology was his two-volume *A Manual of the Ornithology of the United States*

and of Canada, published 1832-1834. A second edition of the first
volume was published in 1840. His name graces the scientific
names of the Poor-will *(Phalaenoptilus nuttallii),* the Nuttall's
Woodpecker *(Picoides nuttallii),* the Yellow-billed Magpie *(Pica
nuttalli),* and our coastal subspecies of the White-crowned Sparrow *(Zonotrichia leucophrys nuttalli),* sometimes called the Nuttall's White-crown.

William Gambel, an American, collected birds in and near
Monterey in 1842 and described from his own material three new
species of birds, the Plain Titmouse, the Wrentit, and the California Thrasher (Gambel, 1845). Fittingly, the California Thrasher,
first illustrated from a Monterey specimen in the *Atlas* of La
Pérouse's voyage in 1797, was formally described 48 years later
from another specimen taken at the same locality. It is Gambel's
name that is perpetuated in the Gambel's White-crown *(Zonotrichia leucophrys gambelii).*

William Hutton, an American who lived in Monterey from
May, 1847, to November, 1848, obtained three specimens of a
vireo which eventually came to John Cassin, curator of birds at
the Philadelphia Academy of Natural Sciences. Cassin (1851)
named these a new species, *Vireo huttoni,* the Hutton's Vireo, in
honor of the collector. This brought the number of new species of
North American birds described from Monterey specimens to its
grand total of eight. The only other California locality to
approach this record was San Francisco, with four new species to
its credit. Santa Cruz and Point Sur were the only other Monterey Bay area localities to provide ornithological novelties, and
each supplied the material for the description of only one
subspecies.

After 1850, ornithological activity in the Monterey Bay area
slacked off considerably. Prévost and Des Murs (1855) reported
on a collection of birds supposedly made by Dr. Néboux, surgeon
of the French frigate *La Vénus,* some of which presumably came
from Monterey. However, as Grinnell (1909) has noted, six of the
11 species supposedly collected at Monterey are tropical, and it

POINT PINOS JUNCO (JUNCO HYEMALIS PINOSUS).

Point Pinos Junco from a plate accompanying an article by Leverett Mills Loomis in *The Auk* of 1894.

seems likely that localities were confused. Grinnell had no confidence in any of these Monterey records, nor do we.

The next ornithologist of note to work in our area was Leverett Mills Loomis. In 1893 he was a student at the Hopkins Seaside Laboratory, better known to us as the Hopkins Marine Station. He formed a warm friendship with Edward Berwick, who allowed Loomis to collect freely on his ranch in the Carmel Valley. In 1894 Loomis accepted the position of Curator of Ornithology at the California Academy of Sciences, and from 1902 to 1912 he served as director of that institution. He did a great deal of work on the marine and pelagic birds of Monterey Bay and published a five-part series, *California Water Birds,* four parts of which described the offshore bird life on Monterey Bay at different seasons of the year (Loomis, 1895, 1896, 1900a,

1900b). He also described the subspecies of Dark-eyed Junco resident in our area, *Junco hyemalis pinosus,* from specimens that he collected at Point Pinos (Loomis, 1893).

Richard C. McGregor published an annotated list of the land birds of Santa Cruz County in 1901, based on his own and others' notes (McGregor, 1901). Later, he served as ornithologist in the Bureau of Science at Manila and became a leading authority on the birds of the Philippine Islands.

Rollo H. Beck, who was in a class by himself as a collector of marine and pelagic birds, collected offshore birds on Monterey Bay for the California Academy of Sciences at various times between 1903 and 1910 and for the Museum of Vertebrate Zoology from August 2, 1910, to April 10, 1911. The unique techniques that Beck used in specimen preparation have been described by Murphy (1936), and some of the high points in the colorful life of this remarkable man were set down in an autobiography which Beck wrote in the same volume at Murphy's request.

Halstead G. White, a graduate student in the Museum of Vertebrate Zoology, made an extensive collection of birds and mammals in the Monterey Peninsula area for that institution between December 11, 1918, and February 20, 1919.

Joseph Grinnell and Jean M. Linsdale, director and research associate, respectively, of the Museum of Vertebrate Zoology, made a detailed survey of the vertebrates of the Point Lobos State Reserve from November 18, 1934, to November 13, 1935, and presented much information on the birds of that area (Grinnell and Linsdale, 1936).

Oscar Perry Silliman of Salinas (1876-1943) put together large collections of birds and mammals from Monterey County, and a large collection of bird eggs; all these specimens went to the Museum of Vertebrate Zoology after Mr. Silliman's death. He is best remembered, however, for his superb library of works in ornithology, mammalogy, and general natural history. This library was bequeathed to Hartnell College and is maintained there as the Silliman Library.

Clark P. Streator (1866-1952) was a long-time resident of Santa Cruz. As a young man he had practiced taxidermy and later he collected birds and mammals for the American Museum of Natural History and for the Bureau of Biological Survey, now the United States Fish and Wildlife Service. During his long residence in Santa Cruz he built up an extensive collection of local birds and mammals which went to the Museum of Vertebrate Zoology after his death.

The late Laidlaw Williams studied the birds of the Monterey Peninsula area extensively from the early 1930s until his death in 1976. He provided a great deal of information on the avifauna of the region. Among his many publications are two lengthy papers on the behavior of the Brandt's Cormorant (Williams, 1942) and the Brewer's Blackbird (Williams, 1952). With Ken Legg and Francis Williamson he described the remarkable nesting of the Parula Warbler at Point Lobos State Reserve (Williams et al., 1958), the first known occurrence of that species in California. He was the unquestioned authority on the birds of the southern Monterey Bay area.

The University of California's Hastings Natural History Reservation was established in the upper Carmel Valley in 1937. Although somewhat removed from Monterey Bay, it has provided ecological and behavioral information on a number of land bird species resident in the Monterey Bay area through the publications of the late Jean M. Linsdale and others.

The Monterey Peninsula Audubon Society was founded in 1943 under the leadership of Laidlaw Williams, who served as president in its first year. Louise Hatton succeeded him. Mr. Williams also organized the society's Check-list Committee and served as its chairman until his death. The society holds meetings every month but July and August, takes numerous field trips during the year, and participates in the Christmas Bird Count. Its publications include *The Sanderling,* which appears every month but July and August, and the *List of the Birds of the Monterey Peninsula Region,* compiled by the Check-list Committee; the latest edition was published in 1977.

The Santa Cruz Bird Club was organized by Elaine Reinelt in 1956, and its first president was Otto Van Buren. The purpose of the club is the study and preservation of birds and their habitats with special reference to Santa Cruz County. Members of the club take a number of field trips each year and participate in the Christmas Bird Count.

Santa Cruz County has become ornithologically famous as the site of discovery of the first nests of two species of North American birds. The first nest and egg of the Black Swift were discovered by the indefatigable and intrepid oologist A. G. Vrooman of Santa Cruz on June 16, 1901, on a cliff a few miles west of that city (Vrooman, 1901). The first North American nest of the Marbled Murrelet, and the first chick of that species known to science, were discovered in Big Basin Redwood State Park on August 7, 1974. The nest, chick, and circumstances of discovery were discussed in detail by Binford et al. (1975).

This completes our brief review of the history of ornithology in the Monterey Bay area from the earliest records to the present. Those interested in pursuing this subject further should consult Grinnell's great three-part *Bibliography of California Ornithology* (Grinnell, 1909, 1924, 1939), an exhaustive listing of the pertinent literature through 1938; Grinnell's *Type Localities of Birds Described from California* (Grinnell, 1932); and T. S. Palmer's useful paper *Notes on Persons Whose Names Appear in the Nomenclature of California Birds* (Palmer, 1928).

Bibliography

Addicott, A.B. 1938. Behavior of the bush-tit in the breeding season. Condor 40:49-63.

Ainley, D.G. 1976. The occurence of seabirds in the coastal region of California. Western Birds 7:33-68.

Ainley, D.G., and T.J. Lewis. 1974. The history of Farallon Island marine bird populations, 1854-1972. Condor 76:432-446.

Ainley, D.G., and G.A. Sanger. 1979. Trophic relations of seabirds in the northeastern Pacific Ocean and Bering Sea. Pages 95-12 in Conservation of Marine Birds of Northern North America, edited by J.C. Bartonek and D.N. Nettleship. U.S. Fish and Wildlife Service. Wildlife Research Report 11.

Ainley, D.G., and M.C. Whitt. 1973. Numbers of marine birds breeding in northern California. Western Birds 4:65-70.

Allen, G.M. 1925. Birds and their attributes. Boston: Marshall Jones Company.

Anderson, W. 1970. A preliminary study of the relationships of salt ponds and wildlife—south San Francisco Bay, California. California Fish and Game 56:240-252.

Anderson, W.L., and R.W. Storer. 1976. Factors influencing Kirtland's warbler nesting success. Jack-Pine Warbler 54:105-115.

Arbib, R. 1973. What the A.O.U. check-list committee has done to your life list. American Birds 27:576-577.

Arbib, R., O.S. Pettingill, Jr., and S.H. Spofford. 1966. Enjoying Birds around New York City. Boston: Houghton Mifflin Co.

Ashmole, N.P. 1971. Seabird ecology and the marine environment. Pages 223-286 in Avian Biology, vol. 1, edited by D.S. Farner and J.R. King. New York: Academic Press.

Baker, M.C., and A.E.M. Baker. 1973. Niche relationships among six species of shorebirds on their wintering and breeding ranges. Ecological Monographs 43:193-212.

Balaguer, O. 1973. A natural history study of the Carmel River marsh, with special reference to vegetation. Mimeographed, not distributed.

Baldridge, A. 1973. The status of the brown pelican in the Monterey region of California: past and present. Western Birds 4:93-100.

Baltz, D.M., and G.V. Morejohn. 1976. Evidence from seabirds of plastic particle pollution off central California. Western Birds 7:111-112.

Baltz, D.M., and G.V. Morejohn. 1977. Food habits and niche overlap of seabirds wintering on Monterey Bay, California. Auk 94:526-543.

Baltz, D.M., G.V. Morejohn, and B.S. Antrim. 1979. Size selective predation and food habits of two California terns. Western Birds 10:17-24.

Banks, R.C. 1959. Development of nestling white-crowned sparrows in central coastal California. Condor 61:96-109.

Beal. F.E.L. 1907. Birds of California in Relation to the Fruit Industry. Part 1. U.S. Department of Agriculture, Biological Survey, Bulletin No. 30.

Beal, F.E.L. 1910. Birds of California in Relation to the Fruit Industry. Part 2. U.S. Department of Agriculture, Biological Survey, Bulletin No. 34.

Beal, F.E.L. 1911. Food of the Woodpeckers of the United States. U.S. Department of Agriculture, Biological Survey, Bulletin No. 37.

Beck, R.H. 1910. Water birds of the vicinity of Point Pinos, California. Proceedings of the California Academy of Sciences, 4th series, 3:57-72.

Bent, A.C. 1937. Life Histories of North American Birds of Prey. Order Falconiformes (Part 1). U.S. National Museum, Bulletin 167.

Binford, L.C., B.G. Elliott, and S.W. Singer. 1975. Discovery of a nest and the downy young of the marbled murrelet. Wilson Bulletin 87:303-319.

Bissonnette, T.H., and A.J. Zujko. 1936. Normal progressive changes in the ovary of the starling (*Sturnus vulgaris*) from December to April. Auk 53: 31-50.

Blanchard, B.D. 1941. The white-crowned sparrows (*Zonotrichia leucophrys*) of the Pacific seaboard: environment and annual cycle. University of California Publications in Zoology 46:1-178.

Blanchard, B.D., and M.M. Erickson. 1949. The cycle in the Gambel sparrow. University of California Publications in Zoology 47:255-318.

Bock, C.E., and L.W. Lepthien. 1974. Winter patterns of bird species diversity and abundance in the United States and southern Canada. American Birds 28:556-562.

Bolin, R.L., and D.P. Abbott. 1963. Studies on the marine climate and phytoplankton of the central coastal area of California, 1954-1960. California Cooperative Oceanic Fisheries Investigations Reports 9:23-45.

Brown, V., H. Weston, Jr., and J. Buzzell. 1973. Handbook of California Birds. Second edition. Healdsburg, California: Naturegraph Publishers.

Bryant, H.C. 1912. Birds in relation to a grasshopper outbreak in California. University of California Publications in Zoology 11:1-20.

Bryant, H.C. 1914. A determination of the economic status of the western meadowlark (*Sturnella neglecta*) in California. University of California Publications in Zoology 11:377-511.

Burton, P.J.K. 1974. Feeding and the Feeding Apparatus in Waders: a Study of Anatomy and Adaptations in the Charadrii. British Museum (Natural History) Publication No. 719.

California Coastal Plan. 1975. Sacramento: California Coastal Zone Conservation Commission.

Cassin, J. 1851. Sketch of the birds composing the genera *Vireo*, Vieillot, and *Vireosylva*, Bonaparte, with a list of the previously known and descriptions of three new species. Proceedings of the Academy of Natural Sciences of Philadelphia 5:149-154.

Cody, M.L. 1968. On the methods of resource division in grassland bird communities. American Naturalist 102:107-147.

Cogswell, H.L. 1977. Water Birds of California. Berkeley: University of California Press.

Cohen, D.A. 1899. Nesting and other habits of the Oregon towhee. Bulletin of the Cooper Ornithological Club 1:61-63.

Corbin, K.W., and C.G. Sibley. 1977. Rapid evolution in orioles of the genus *Icterus*. Condor 79:335-342.

Couch, A.B. 1966. Feeding Ecology of Four Species of Sandpipers in Western Washington. M.A. dissertation, University of Washington, Seattle.

Coues, E. 1874. Birds of the Northwest. U.S. Geological Survey of the Territories, Miscellaneous Publications, No. 3.

Cowan, J.B. 1952. Life history and productivity of a population of western mourning doves in California. California Fish and Game 38:505-521.

Cox, G.W. 1968. The role of competition in the evolution of migration. Evolution 22:180-192.

Davis, J. 1951. Distribution and variation of the brown towhees. University of California Publications in Zoology 52:1-120.

Davis, J. 1957. Comparative foraging behavior of the spotted and brown towhees. Auk 74:129-166.

Davis, J. 1958. Singing behavior and the gonad cycle of the rufous-sided towhee. Condor 60:308-336.

Davis, J. 1971. Breeding and molt schedules of the rufous-collared sparrow in coastal Perú. Condor 73:127-146.

Davis, M.E. 1974. Experiments on the nesting behavior of the Least Tern, *Sterna albifrons browni*. Proceedings of the Linnaean Society of New York 72:25-43.

Davis, J., G.F. Fisler, and B.S. Davis. 1963. The breeding biology of the western flycatcher. Condor 65:337-382.

Davis, J., and L. Williams. 1957. Irruptions of the Clark nutcracker in California. Condor 59:297-307.

Davis, J., and L. Williams. 1964. The 1961 irruption of the Clark's nutcracker in California. Wilson Bulletin 76:10-18.

Dawson, W.L. 1923. The Birds of California. Sunset Edition De Luxe. San Diego: South Moulton Co.

Dawson, W.L., and J.H. Bowles. 1909. The Birds of Washington. Original Edition. Seattle: The Occidental Publishing Company.

Dawson, W.R., and F.C. Evans. 1957. Relation of growth and development to temperature regulation in nestling field and chipping sparrows. Physiological Zoology 30:315-327.

Dawson, W.R., and F.C. Evans. 1960. Relation of growth and development to temperature regulation in nestling vesper sparrows. Condor 62:329-340.

Diamond, J.M. 1978. Niche shifts and the rediscovery of interspecific competition. American Scientist 66:322-331.

Dilger, W.C. 1956. Hostile behavior and reproductive isolating mechanisms in the avian genera *Catharus* and *Hylocichla*. Auk 73:313-353.

Dixon, K.L. 1963. Some aspects of social organization in the Carolina chickadee. Proceedings of the 13th International Ornithological Congress: 240-258.

Dolnik, V.R., and T.I. Blyumenthal. 1967. Autumnal premigratory and migratory periods in the chaffinch (*Fringilla coelebs coelebs*) and some other temperate-zone birds. Condor 69:435-468.

Drent, R.H. 1965. Breeding biology of the pigeon guillemot, *Cepphus columba*. Ardea 53:99-160.

Drent, R.H. 1975. Incubation. Pages 333-420 *in* Avian Biology, vol. 5, edited by D.S. Farner and J.R. King. New York: Academic Press.

Dunn, E.H., 1975. The timing of endothermy in the development of altricial birds. Condor 77:288-293.

Dwight, J., Jr. 1900. The sequence of plumages and moults of the passerine birds of New York. Annals of the New York Academy of Sciences 13:73-360.

Elliott, P.F. 1977. Adaptive significance of cowbird egg distribution. Auk 94:590-593.

Eltringham, S.K. 1971. Life in Mud and Sand. London: English Universities Press Limited.

Emlen, J.T., Jr. 1952. Social behavior in nesting cliff swallows. Condor 54:177-199.

Emlen, J.T. 1974. An urban bird community in Tucson, Arizona: derivation, structure, regulation. Condor 76:184-197.

Emlen, S.T. 1967a. Migratory orientation in the indigo bunting, *Passerina cyanea*. Part 1: evidence for use of celestial cues. Auk 84:309-342.

Emlen, S.T. 1967b. Migratory orientation in the indigo bunting, *Passerina cyanea*. Part 2: mechanism of celestial orientation. Auk 84:463-489.

Emlen, S.T. 1975. Migration: orientation and navigation. Pages 129-219 *in* Avian Biology, vol. 5, edited by D.S. Farner and J.R. King. New York: Academic Press.

Emlen, S.T., and J.T. Emlen. 1966. A technique for recording migratory orientation of captive birds. Auk 83:361-367.

Engels, W.L. 1940. Structural adaptations in thrashers (Mimidae: genus *Toxostoma*) with comments on interspecific relationships. University of California Publications in Zoology 42:341-400.

Erickson, M.M. 1938. Territory, annual cycle, and numbers in a population of wren-tits (*Chamaea fasciata*). University of California Publications in Zoology 42:247-334.

Falls, J.B. 1969. Functions of territorial song in the white-throated sparrow. Pages 207-232 *in* Bird Vocalizations, edited by R.A. Hinde. Cambridge: Cambridge University Press.

Farner, D.S. 1955. The annual stimulus for migration: experimental and physiologic aspects. Pages 198-237 *in* Recent Studies in Avian Biology, edited by A. Wolfson. Urbana: University of Illinois Press.

Foster, M.S. 1967. Molt cycles of the orange-crowned warbler. Condor 69: 169-200.

Fretwell, S. 1968. Habitat distribution and survival in the field sparrow (*Spizella pusilla*). Bird-Banding 39:293-306.

Fretwell, S. 1969. Dominance behavior and winter habitat distribution in juncos (*Junco hyemalis*). Bird-Banding 40:1-25.

Fry, C.H. 1972. The social organization of bee-eaters (Meropidae) and co-operative breeding in hot-climate birds. Ibis 114:1-14.

Gambel, W. 1845. Descriptions of new and little known birds collected in Upper California. Proceedings of the Academy of Natural Sciences of Philadelphia 2:263-266.

Gavareski, C.A. 1976. Relation of park size and vegetation to urban bird populations in Seattle, Washington. Condor 78:375-382.

Glynn, P.W. 1961. First recorded mass stranding of pelagic red crabs, *Pleuroncodes planipes,* at Monterey Bay, California, since 1859, with notes on their biology. California Fish and Game 47:97-101.

Glynn, P.W. 1965. Community composition, structure and interrelationships in the marine intertidal *Endocladia muricata-Balanus glandula* association in Monterey Bay, California. Beaufortia 12, No. 148.

Gordon, B.L. 1977. Monterey Bay Area: Natural History and Cultural Imprints. 2nd edition. Pacific Grove, California: Boxwood Press.

Goss-Custard, J.D. 1970. Dispersion in some overwintering wading birds. Pages 3-35 *in* Social Behavior in Birds and Mammals, edited by J.H. Crook. London: Academic Press.

Green, J. 1968. Biology of Estuarine Animals. Seattle: University of Washington Press.

Griffin, J.R. 1971. Oak regeneration in the upper Carmel Valley, California. Ecology 52:862-868.

Griffin, J.R. 1973. Valley oaks—the end of an era? Fremontia 1:5-9.

Griffin, J.R. 1974. Notes on environment, vegetation, and flora, Hastings Natural History Reservation. Mimeographed report on file, Hastings Reservation, Carmel Valley, California.

Griffin, J.R. 1975. Plants of the Highest Santa Lucia and Diablo Range Peaks, California. Pacific Southwest Forest and Range Experiment Station Research Paper PSW - 110.

Griffin, J.R. 1976. Regeneration in *Quercus lobata* savannas, Santa Lucia Mountains, California. American Midland Naturalist 95:422-435.

Griffin, J.R. 1977. Oak woodland. Pages 383-415 *in* Terrestrial Vegetation of California, edited by M.G. Barbour and J. Major. New York: John Wiley & Sons, Inc.

Griffin, J.R., and W.B. Critchfield. 1972. The Distribution of Forest Trees in California. Pacific Southwest Forest and Range Experiment Station Research Paper PSW - 82.

Grinnell, J. 1909. A Bibliography of California Ornithology. Pacific Coast Avifauna No. 5.

Grinnell, J. 1924. Bibliography of California Ornithology. Second Installment. Pacific Coast Avifauna No. 16.

Grinnell, J. 1932. Type localities of birds described from California. University of California Publications in Zoology 38: 243-324.

Grinnell, J. 1936. Uphill planters. Condor 38:80-82.

Grinnell, J. 1939. Bibliography of California Ornithology. Third Installment. Pacific Coast Avifauna No. 26.

Grinnell, J., J.M. Dixon, and J.M. Linsdale. 1930. Vertebrate Natural History of a Section of Northern California through the Lassen Peak Region. Berkeley: University of California Press.

Grinnell, J., and J.M. Linsdale. 1936. Vertebrate Animals of Point Lobos Reserve. Carnegie Institution of Washington Publication No. 481.

Grinnell, J., and A.H. Miller. 1944. The Distribution of the Birds of California. Pacific Coast Avifauna No. 27.

Grinnell, J., and T.I. Storer. 1924. Animal Life in the Yosemite. Berkeley: University of California Press.

Grubb, T.C. 1972. Smell and foraging in shearwaters and petrels. Nature (London) 237:404-405.

Guth, R.W. 1979. Breeding bird survey transect of Chicago metropolitan area, Illinois. Chicago Academy of Sciences, Natural History Miscellanea No. 206.

Hamilton, R.B. 1975. Comparative Behavior of the American Avocet and the Black-necked Stilt (Recurvirostridae). American Ornithologists' Union, Ornithological Monograph No. 17.

Hanna, W.C. 1924. Weights of about three thousand eggs. Condor 26:146-153.

Hartwick, E.B. 1976. Foraging strategy of the black oyster catcher (*Haematopus bachmani* A.). Canadian Journal of Zoology 54:142-155.

Hoffman, W., W.P. Elliott, and J.M. Scott. 1975. The occurrence and status of the horned puffin in the western United States. Western Birds 6:87-94.

Holmes, R.T. 1966. Breeding ecology and annual cycle adaptations of the redbacked sandpiper (*Calidris alpina*) in northern Alaska. Condor 68:3-46.

Howell, T.R. 1953. Racial and sexual differences in migration in *Sphyrapicus varius*. Auk 70:118-126.

Howitt, B.F. 1972. Floral areas. Pages 7-11 *in* Forest Heritage: A Natural History of the Del Monte Forest. Compiled by B.F. Howitt. Berkeley: California Native Plant Society.

Howitt, B.F., and J.T. Howell. 1964. The vascular plants of Monterey County, California. Wasmann Journal of Biology 22:1-184.

Humphrey, P.S., and K.C. Parkes. 1959. An approach to the study of molts and plumages. Auk 76:1-31.

Johnson, A.W. 1904. Notes on unusual nesting sites of the Pacific yellowthroat. Condor 6:129-131.

Johnson, N.K. 1963. Comparative molt cycles in the tyrannid genus *Empidonax*. Proceedings of the 13th International Ornithological Congress: 870-883.

Johnson, N.K. 1974. Molt and age determination in western and yellowish flycatchers. Auk 91:111-131.

Johnston, D.W., and R.W. McFarlane. 1967. Migration and bioenergetics of flight in the Pacific golden plover. Condor 69:156-168.

Johnston, R.F. 1954. Variation in breeding season and clutch size in song sparrows of the Pacific coast. Condor 56:268-273.

Judd, S.D. 1901. The Relation of Sparrows to Agriculture. U.S. Department of Agriculture, Biological Survey, Bulletin No. 15.

Kelly, J.W. 1955. History of the nesting of an Anna hummingbird. Condor 57:347-353.

Kendeigh, S.C. 1952. Parental care and its evolution in birds. Illinois Biolocial Monographs 22 (1-3):1-356.

Kenyon, K.W., and D.W. Rice. 1958. Homing of Laysan albatrosses. Condor 60:3-6.

King, J.R. 1955. Notes on the life history of Traill's flycatcher (*Empidonax traillii*) in southeastern Washington. Auk 72:148-173.

King, J.R., and D.S. Farner. 1961. Energy metabolism, thermoregulation and body temperature. Pages 215-288 *in* Biology and Comparative Physiology of Birds, vol. 2, edited by A.J. Marshall. New York: Academic Press.

King, W.B., R.G.B. Brown, and G.A. Sanger. 1979. Mortality to marine birds through commerical fishing. Pages 195-199 *in* Conservation of Marine Birds of Northern North America, edited by J.C. Bartonek and D.N. Nettleship. U.S. Fish and Wildlife Service, Wildlife Research Report No. 11.

Kramer, G. 1950. Orientierte Zugaktivität gekäftiger Singvögel. Naturwissenschaften 37:188.

Kramer, G. 1951. Eine neue Methode zur Erforschung der Zugorientierung und die bisher damit erzielten Ergebnisse. Proceedings of the 10th International Ornithological Congress:269-280.

Lack, D. 1947. The significance of clutch size. Ibis 89:302-352.

Lack, D. 1958. The significance of the colour of turdine eggs. Ibis 100:145-166.

Lack, D. 1968. Ecological adaptations for breeding in birds. London: Methuen & Co. Ltd.

La Rivers, I. 1941. The Mormon cricket as food for birds. Condor 43:65-69.

Larkin, R.P., and P.J. Sutherland. 1977. Migrating birds respond to Project Seafarer's electromagnetic field. Science 195:777-779.

Lawrence, L. de K. 1967. A Comparative Life-history Study of Four Species of Woodpeckers. American Ornithologists' Union, Ornithological Monograph No. 5.

Legg, K. 1954. Nesting and feeding of the black oyster-catcher near Monterey, California. Condor 56:359-360.

Limbaugh, C. 1955. Fish life in the Kelp Beds and the Effect of Harvesting. University of California Institute of Marine Sciences, IMR Reference 55-9:1-158.

Linsdale, J.M. 1937. The Natural History of Magpies. Pacific Coast Avifauna No. 25.

Linsdale, J.M. 1942. San Francisco region. Audubon Magazine 44 (2), Section 2:14-15.

Linsdale, J.M. 1947. A ten-year record of bird occurrence on the Hastings Reservation. Condor 49:236-241.

Linsdale, J.M. 1957. Goldfinches on the Hastings Natural History Reservation. American Midland Naturalist 57:1-119.

Linsdale, J.M., and E.L. Sumner, Sr. 1934. Winter weights of golden-crowned and fox sparrows. Condor 36:107-112.

Linsdale, J.M., and P.Q. Tomich. 1953. A Herd of Mule Deer. Berkeley: University of California Press.

Loomis, L.M. 1893. Description of a new junco from California. Auk 10:47-48.

Loomis, L.M. 1895. California Water Birds. No. 1. Monterey and vicinity from the middle of June to the end of August. Proceedings of the California Academy of Sciences, 2nd series, 5:177-224.

Loomis, L.M. 1896. California water birds. No. 2. Vicinity of Monterey in midwinter. Proceedings of the California Academy of Sciences, 2nd series, 6:1-30.

Loomis, L.M. 1900a. California water birds. No. 4. Vicinity of Monterey in autumn. Proceedings of the California Academy of Sciences, 3rd series, 2:277-322.

Loomis, L.M. 1900b. California water birds. No. 5. Vicinity of Monterey in May and early June. Proceedings of the California Academy of Sciences, 3rd series, 2:349-363.

Lussenhop, J. 1977. Urban cemeteries as bird refuges. Condor 79:456-461.

Macdonald, K.B. 1977. Coastal salt marsh. Pages 263-294 in Terrestrial Vegetation of California, edited by M.G. Barbour and J. Major. New York: John Wiley & Sons, Inc.

MacRoberts, M.H., and B.R. MacRoberts. 1976. Social Organization and Behavior of the Acorn Woodpecker in Central Coastal California. American Ornithologists' Union, Ornithological Monograph No. 21.

Marler, P. 1956. Behaviour of the Chaffinch Fringilla coelebs. Behaviour, Supplement 5.

Marler, P. 1970. A comparative approach to vocal learning: song development in white-crowned sparrows. Journal of Comparative Physiology and Psychology Monograph 71, No. 2, part 2:1-25.

Marler, P., and D. Isaac. 1960. Song variation in a population of brown towhees. Condor 62:272-283.

Marler, P., and S. Peters. 1977. Selective vocal learning in a sparrow. Science 198:519-521.

Marler, P., and M. Tamura. 1964. Culturally transmitted patterns of vocal behavior in sparrows. Science 146:1483-1486.

Martin, A.C., H.S. Zim, and A.L. Nelson. 1961. American Wildlife & Plants. New York: Dover Publications, Inc.

Massey, B.W. 1974. Breeding biology of the California Least Tern. Proceedings of the Linnaean Society of New York 72:1-24.

Mayfield, H. 1961. Cowbird parasitism and the population of the Kirtland's warbler. Evolution 15:174-179.

Mayfield, H. 1965. Chance distribution of cowbird eggs. Condor 67:257-263.

Mayr, E. 1940. Speciation phenomena in birds. American Naturalist 74:249-278.

Mayr, E., and L.L. Short. 1970. Species Taxa of North American Birds. Publications of the Nuttall Ornithological Club, No. 9.

McAtee, W.L. 1905. The Horned Larks and Their Relation to Agriculture. U.S. Department of Agriculture, Biological Survey, Bulletin 23.

McGinitie, G.E. 1935. Ecological aspects of a California marine estuary. American Midland Naturalist 16:629-765.

McGinitie, G.E., and N. McGinitie. 1968. Natural History of Marine Animals. New York: McGraw-Hill Book Company.

McGregor, R.C. 1901. A List of the Land Birds of Santa Cruz County, California. Pacific Coast Avifauna No. 2.

Mewaldt, L.R. 1952. The incubation patch of the Clark nutcracker. Condor 54:361.

Mewaldt, L.R. 1956. Nesting behavior of the Clark nutcracker. Condor 58:3-23.

Mewaldt, L.R., M.L. Morton, and I.L. Brown. 1964. Orientation of migratory restlessness in *Zonotrichia*. Condor 66:377-417.

Michener, H., and J.R. Michener. 1935. Mockingbirds, their territories and individualities. Condor 37:97-140.

Michener, H., and J.R. Michener. 1943. The spring molt of the Gambel sparrow. Condor 45:113-116.

Milet-Mureau, M.L.A. 1797. Voyage de La Pérouse autour du monde, Publié Conformément au Décret du 22 Avril, 1797, et Rédigé par M.L.A. Milet-Mureau. Vol. 2. Paris: de l'imprimerie de la Republique. Also, Atlas du Voyage de La Pérouse.

Milet-Mureau, M.L.A. 1798. A Voyage round the World, in the Years 1785, 1786, 1787, and 1788, by J.F.G. de La Pérouse, ... and edited by M.L.A. Milet-Mureau. Vol. 2. London: J. Johnson.

Miller, A.H. 1932. The passerine fossil birds from the Pleistocene of Carpinteria, California. University of California Publications, Bulletin of the Department of Geological Sciences 21:169-194.

Miller, A.H. 1941. Speciation in the avian genus *Junco*. University of California Publications in Zoology 44:173-434.

Miller, A.H. 1951. An analysis of the distribution of the birds of California. University of California Publications in Zoology 50:531-644.

Miller, A.H. 1962. Bimodal occurrence of breeding in an equatorial sparrow. Proceedings of the National Academy of Sciences 48: 396-400.

Miller, A.H., and R.C. Stebbins. 1964. The Lives of Desert Animals in Joshua Tree National Monument. Berkeley: University of California Press.

Moffitt, J. 1941. Notes on the food of the California clapper rail. Condor 43:270-273.

Morejohn, G.V. 1978. First North American record of the streaked shearwater (*Puffinus leucomelas*). Auk 95:420.

Morejohn, G.V., J.T. Harvey, and L.T. Krasnow. 1978. The importance of *Loligo opalescens* in the food web of marine vertebrates in Monterey Bay, California. California Department of Fish and Game, Fish Bulletin 169:67-98.

Morton, M.L., J.R. King, and D.S. Farner. 1969. Postnuptial and postjuvenal molt in white-crowned sparrows in central Alaska. Condor 71:376-385.

Munz, P.A. 1963. A California Flora. Berkeley: University of California Press.

Murphy, R.C. 1925. Bird Islands of Peru. New York: G.F. Putnam's Sons.

Murphy, R.C.. 1936. Oceanic Birds of South America. New York: The American Museum of Natural History.

Myers, J.P., P.G. Connors, and F.A. Pitelka. 1979a. Territoriality in nonbreeding shorebirds. Pages 231-246 in Shorebirds in Marine Environments, edited by F.A. Pitelka. Studies in Avian Biology No. 2.

Myers, J.P., P.G. Connors, and F.A. Pitelka. 1979b. Territory size in wintering sanderlings: the effects of prey abundance and intruder density. Auk 96:551-561.

Nelson, R.W., and M.T. Myres. 1976. Decline in populations of peregrine falcons and their seabird prey at Langara Island, British Columbia. Condor 78:281-293.

Nice, M.M. 1937. Studies in the life history of the song sparrow I. Transactions of the Linnaean Society of New York, vol. 4.

Nice, M.M. 1943. Studies in the life history of the song sparrow II. Transactions of the Linnaean Society of New York, vol. 6.

Odum, E.P., C.E. Connell, and H.L. Stoddard. 1961. Flight energy and estimated flight ranges of some migratory birds. Auk 78:515-527.

Orians, G.H. 1961. The ecology of blackbird (*Agelaius*) social systems. Ecological Monographs 31:285-312.

Orians, G.H., and G.M. Christman. 1968. A comparative study of the behavior of red-winged, tricolored, and yellow-headed blackbirds. University of California Publications in Zoology 84:1-85.

Orr, R.T. 1942. A study of the birds of the Big Basin region of California. American Midland Naturalist 27:273-337.

Owens, N.W., and J.D. Goss-Custard. 1976. The adaptive significance of alarm calls given by shorebirds on their winter feeding grounds. Evolution 30:397-398.

Page, G.B., B. Fearis, and R.M. Jurek. 1972. Age and sex composition of western sandpipers on Bolinas Lagoon. California Birds 3:79-86.

Page, G.B., and D.F. Whiteacre. 1975. Raptor predation on wintering shorebirds. Condor 77:73-83.

Palmer, R.S. (editor). 1962. Handbook of North American Birds, vol. 1. Loons through Flamingos. New Haven: Yale University Press.

Palmer, R.S. (editor) 1976. Handbook of North American Birds, vols 2 and 3. Waterfowl, Parts 1 and 2. New Haven: Yale University Press.

Palmer, T.S. 1928. Notes on persons whose names appear in the nomenclature of California birds. Condor 30:261-307.

Parkes, K.C. 1975. Special review. Auk 92:818-830.

Payne, R.B. 1972. Mechanisms and control of molt. Pages 103-155, in Avian Biology, vol.2, edited by D.S. Farner and J.R. King. New York: Academic Press.

Payne, R.B. 1976. The clutch size and numbers of eggs of brown-headed cowbirds: effects of latitude and breeding season. Condor 78:337-342.

Pearse, J.S., and V.A. Gerard. 1977. Kelp forests. Pages 645-649 in Coastal Ecosystem Management, edited by J.R. Clark. New York: John Wiley & Sons, Inc.

Peterson, R.T. 1961. A Field Guide to Western Birds. Boston: Houghton Mifflin Co.

Phillips, C.L. 1887. Egg-laying extraordinary in Colaptes. Auk 4:346.

Pitelka, F.A. 1951. Speciation and and ecologic distribution in American jays of the genus Aphelocoma. University of California Publications in Zoology 50:195-464.

Pitelka, F.A. 1958. Timing of molt in Steller jays of the Queen Charlotte Islands, British Columbia. Condor 60:38-49.

Pitelka, F.A. 1959. Numbers, breeding schedule, and territoriality in pectoral sandpipers of northern Alaska. Condor 61:233-264.

Pitelka, F.A. (editor). 1979. Shorebirds in Marine Environments. Studies in Avian Biology No. 2.

Pleszczynska, W.K. 1978. Microgeographic prediction of polygyny in the lark bunting. Science 201:935-936.

Pray, R.H. 1954. Middle Pacific coast region. Audubon Field Notes 8: 326-327.

Prévost, F., and O. Des Murs. 1855. Oiseaux. Pages 177-279 in Voyage autour du Monde sur la Frégate La Vénus. Mammifères, Oiseaux, Reptiles, et Poissons. Paris: Gide et J. Baudry. [Reference not seen by us]

Pulich, W.M. 1976. The Golden-cheeked Warbler. Austin: Texas Parks and Wildlife Department.

Pulliam, H.R., and G.S. Mills. 1977. The use of space by wintering sparrows. Ecology 58:1393-1399.

Purdue, J.R. 1975. Adaptations of the snowy plover, Charadrius alexandrinus, to an inland salt plain. Dissertation Abstracts 35B:4428 (No. 75-6549).

Quaintance, C.W. 1938. Content, meaning, and possible origin of male song in the brown towhee. Condor 40:97-101.

Quast, J.C. 1971a. Fish fauna of the rocky inshore zone. Pages 481-507 in The Biology of Giant Kelp Beds (Macrocystis) in California, edited by W.J. North. Beihefte zur Nova Hedwegia. Heft 32. Lehre, Germany:J. Cramer.

Quast, J.C. 1971b. Estimates of the populations and the standing crop of kelp bed fishes. Pages 509-540 in Ibid.

Radovich, J. 1961. Relationship of some marine organisms of the northeast Pacific to water temperatures, particularly during 1957 through 1959. California Department of Fish and Game, Fish Bulletin 112.

Rahn, H., and A. Ar. 1974. The avian egg: incubation time and water loss. Condor 76:147-152.

Recher, H.F. 1966. Some aspects of the ecology of migrant shorebirds. Ecology 47:393-407.

Recher, H.F., and J.A. Recher. 1969. Some aspects of the ecology of migrant shorebirds. II. Aggression. Wilson Bulletin 81:140-154.

Reeder, W.G. 1951. Stomach analysis of a group of shorebirds. Condor 53:43-45.

Remsen, J.V., and L.C. Binford. 1975. Status of the yellow-billed loon, *Gavia adamsii*, in the western United States and Mexico. Western Birds 6:1-6.

Ricketts, E.F., and J. Calvin. 1968. Between Pacific Tides. 4th edition. Revised by J.W. Hedgepeth. Stanford, California: Stanford University Press.

Ricklefs, R.E., and F.R. Hainsworth. 1968. Temperature regulation in nestling cactus wrens: the development of homeothermy. Condor 70:121-127.

Risebrough, R.W., D.B. Menzel, D.J. Martin, and H.S. Olcott. 1967. DDT residues in Pacific sea birds; a persistent insecticide in marine food chains. Nature (London) 216:589-591.

Robbins, C.S., B. Bruun, and H.S. Zim. 1966. Birds of North America. New York: Golden Press.

Rothstein, S.I. 1975. An experimental and teleonomic investigation of avian brood parasitism. Condor 77:250-271.

Rowan, W. 1925. Relation of light to bird migration and developmental changes. Nature (London) 115:494-495.

Rowan, W. 1926. On photoperiodism, reproductive periodicity, and the annual migrations of birds and certain fishes. Proceedings of the Boston Society of Natural History 38:147-189.

Sabine, W.S. 1955. The winter society of the Oregon junco: the flock. Condor 57:88-111.

Sabine, W.S. 1959. The winter society of the Oregon junco: intolerance, dominance, and the pecking order. Condor 61:110-135.

Sargent, G.T. 1940. Observations on the behavior of color-banded California thrashers. Condor 42:49-60.

Sauer, F. 1957. Die sternenorientierung mächtlich ziehender Grasmücken (*Sylvia atricapilla, borin,* und *curruca*). Zeitschrift für Tierpsychologie 14:29-70.

Sawyer, J.O., D.A. Thornburgh, and J.R. Griffin. 1977. Mixed evergreen forest. Pages 359-381 *in* Terrestrial Vegetation of California, edited by M.G. Barbour and J. Major. New York: John Wiley & Sons, Inc.

Schmidt-Nielsen, K., and R. Fange. 1958. The function of the salt gland in the brown pelican. Auk 75:282-289.

Schmidt-Nielsen, K., C.B. Jörgensen, and H. Osaki. 1958. Extrarenal salt excretion in birds. American Journal of Physiology 193:101-107.

Schmidt-Nielsen, K., and W.J.L. Sladen. 1958. Nasal salt secretion in the Humboldt penguin. Nature (London) 181:1217-1218.

Schneider, D. 1978. Equalisation by prey numbers of migratory shorebirds. Nature (London) 271:353-354.

Selander, R.K., and D.R. Giller. 1961. Analysis of sympatry of great-tailed and boat-tailed grackles. Condor 63:29-86.

Shaw, G., and F.P. Nodder. 1797. The Naturalist's Miscellany, vol. 9. Plate 301 and text; Plate 345 and text. London: Nodder and Company.

Shoemaker, V.H. 1972. Osmoregulation and excretion in birds. Pages 527-574 *in* Avian Biology, vol. 2, edited by D.S. Farner and J.R. King. New York: Academic Press.

Sibley, C.G., and L.L. Short, Jr. 1964. Hybridization in the orioles of the Great Plains. Condor 66:130-150.

Silliman, O.P. 1915. Range of the California clapper rail. Condor 17:201.

Simmons, K.E.L. 1972. Some adaptive features of seabird plumage types. British Birds 65:465-479, 510-521.

Skutch, A.F. 1976. Parent Birds and Their Young. Austin: University of Texas Press.

Small, A. 1974. The Birds of California. New York: Winchester Press.

Southern, W.E. 1975. Orientation of gull chicks exposed to Project Sanguine's electromagnetic field. Science 189:143-145.

Stallcup, R.W. 1976. Pelagic birds of Monterey Bay, California. Western Birds 7:113-136.

Stejneger, L. 1886. On the status of *Synthliboramphus wumizusume* as a North American bird. Proceedings of the U.S. National Museum 9:524.

Stendell, R.C., and P. Myers. 1973. White-tailed kite predation on a fluctuating vole population. Condor 75:359-360.

Stenzel, L.E., H.R. Huber, and G.W. Page. 1976. Feeding behavior and diet of the long-billed curlew and willet. Wilson Bulletin 88:314-332.

Storer, R.W. 1951. Variation in the painted bunting (*Passerina ciris*), with speical reference to wintering populations. Occasional Papers of the Museum of Zoology, University of Michigan, No. 532.

Stott, R.S., and D.P. Olson. 1973. Food-habit relationships of sea ducks on the New Hampshire coastline. Ecology 54:996-1007.

Stout, G.D. (editor). 1967. The Shorebirds of North America. New York: Viking Press.

Sutton, G.M. 1938. Oddly plumaged orioles from western Oklahoma. Auk 55:1-6.

Sutton, G.M. 1951. Dispersal of mistletoe by birds. Wilson Bulletin 63:235-237.

Thomas, J.H. 1961. Flora of the Santa Cruz Mountains of California. Stanford, California: Stanford University Press.

Thorne, R.F. 1976. The vascular plant communities of California. Pages 1-31 *in* Plant Communities of Southern California, edited by J. Latting. California Native Plant Society Special Publication No. 2.

Thrailkill, J.R. 1963. Zooplankton Volumes off the Pacific Coast, 1959. U.S. Fish and Wildlife Service, Special Scientific Report—Fisheries, No. 414.

Tinbergen, N. 1935. Field observations of East Greenland birds. I. The behaviour of the red-necked phalarope (*Phalaropus lobatus* L.) in spring. Ardea 24:1-42.

Tinbergen, N. 1939. The behavior of the snow bunting in spring. Transactions of the Linnaean Society of New York, Vol. 5.

Varoujean, D.H. 1973. A Study of the California Clapper Rail in Elkhorn Slough, 1972. California Department of Fish and Game, Special Wildlife Investigation Project. W-54-R-4. Final Report, Job 11.

Varoujean, D.H., and L.J.V. Campagno. 1973. Magnificent frigatebirds in Monterey Bay, California. Auk 90:192-193.

Verbeek, N.A.M. 1973. The exploitation system of the yellow-billed magpie. University of California Publications in Zoology 99:1-58.

Verner, J. 1964. Evolution of polygamy in the long-billed marsh wren. Evolution 18:252-261.

Verner, J. 1965. Breeding biology of the long-billed marsh wren. Condor 67:6-30.

Verner, J., and G.H. Engelsen. 1970. Territories, multiple nest building, and polygyny in the long-billed marsh wren. Auk 87:557-567.

Verner, J., and M.F. Willson. 1966. The influence of habitats on mating systems of North American passerine birds. Ecology 47:143-147.

Vigors, N. 1829. On some species of birds from the north-west coast of America. Zoological Journal 4:352-358.

Vigors, N. 1839. Ornithology. Pages 13-40 in The Zoology of Captain Beechey's Voyage ... in His Majesty's Ship Blossom. London: Henry G. Bohn.

Vince, M.A. 1969. Embryonic communication, respiration and the synchronization of hatching. Pages 233-260 in Bird Vocalizations, edited by R.A. Hinde. Cambridge: Cambridge University Press.

Vogl, R.J., W.P. Armstrong, K.L. White, and K.L. Cole. 1977. The closed-cone pines and cypresses. Pages 295-358 in Terrestrial Vegetation of California. Edited by M.G. Barbour and J. Major. New York: John Wiley & Sons, Inc.

von Haartman, L. 1971. Population dynamics. Pages 391-459 in Avian Biology, vol. 1., edited by D.S. Farner and J.R. King. New York: Academic Press.

Vrooman, A.G. 1901. Discovery of the egg of the black swift (*Cypseloides niger borealis*). Auk 18:394-395.

Vrooman, A.G. 1905. Discovery of a second egg of the black swift. Condor 7:176-177.

Walcott, C., J.L. Gould, and J.L. Kirschvink. 1979. Pigeons have magnets. Science 205:1027-1029.

Walkinshaw, L.H. 1972. Kirtland's warbler—endangered. American Birds 26:3-9.

Ward, P., and A. Zahavi. 1973. The importance of certain assemblages of birds as "information centres" for food-finding. Ibis 115:517-534.

Warter, J.K. 1976. Late Pleistocene plant communities—evidence from the Rancho La Brea tar pits. Pages 32-39 in Plant Communities of Southern California, edited by J. Latting. California Native Plant Society Special Publication No. 2.

Webster, J.D. 1941. Feeding habits of the black oyster-catcher. Condor 43:175-180.

Welter, W.A. 1935. The natural history of the long-billed marsh wren. Wilson Bulletin 47:3-34.

Weston, H.G., Jr. 1947. Breeding behavior of the black-headed grosbeak. Condor 49:54-73.

White, K.L. 1966. Structure and composition of foothill woodland in central coastal California. Ecology 47:229-237.

White, K.L. 1967. Native bunchgrass (*Stipa pulchra*) on Hastings Reservation, California. Ecology 48:949-955.

Wiens, J.A. 1969. An Approach to the Study of Ecological Relationships among Grassland Birds. American Ornithologists' Union, Ornithological Monograph No. 8.

Wiens, J.A., and J.M. Scott. 1975. Model estimations of energy flow in Oregon coastal seabird populations. Condor 77:439-452.

Wilbur, S.R. 1974. The Literature of the California Least Tern. U.S. Fish and Wildlife Service SSR-Wildlife No. 175.

Williams, L. 1927. Brown pelicans nesting at Point Lobos, Monterey County, California. Condor 29:246-249.

Williams, L. 1929. Notes on the feeding habits and behavior of the California clapper rail. Condor 31:52-56.

Williams, L. 1942. Display and sexual behavior of the Brandt Cormorant. Condor 44:85-104.

Williams, L. 1952. Breeding behavior of the Brewer blackbird. Condor 54:3-47.

Williams, L., K. Legg, and F.S.L. Williamson. 1958. Breeding of the parula warbler at Point Lobos, California. Condor 60:345-354.

Wittenberger, J.F. 1976. The ecological factors selecting for polygyny in altricial birds. American Naturalist 110:779-799.

Wolff, W.J. 1973. The Estuary as a Habitat. An Analysis of Data on the Soft-bottom Macrofauna of the Estuarine Area of the Rivers Rhine, Meuse, and Scheldt. Zoologische Verhandelingen No. 126.

Wolfson, A. 1940. A preliminary report on some experiments on bird migration. Condor 42:93-99.

Wolfson, A. 1942. Regulation of spring migration in juncos. Condor 44:237-263.

Woolfenden, G.E. 1975. Florida scrub jay helpers at the nest. Auk 92:1-15.

Woolfenden, G.E., and S.A. Rohwer. 1969a. Breeding birds in Florida suburb. Bulletin of the Florida State Museum 13:1-83.

Woolfenden, G.E., and S.A. Rohwer. 1969b. Bird populations in the suburbs and two woodland habitats, in Pinellas County, Florida. Pages 101-117 in Florida State Board of Health Monograph No. 12.

Yadon, V.L. 1970a. Four thick-billed murre records for Monterey Bay. California Birds 1:107-110.

Yadon, V.L. 1970b. Oceanodroma tethys kelsalli, new to North America. Auk 87:588-589.

Yeagley, H.L. 1947. A preliminary study of a physical basis of bird navigation. Journal of Applied Physics 18:1035-1063.

Yocum, C.F., and M. Keller. 1961. Correlation of food habits and abundance of waterfowl, Humboldt Bay, California. California Fish and Game 47:41-53.

Youngbluth, M.J. 1976. Vertical distribution and diel migration of euphausiids in the central region of the California Current. U.S. Department of Commerce, National Marine Fisheries Service, Fishery Bulletin 74:925-936.

APPENDIX A

Common and Scientific Names for Animals

Mammals

Badger	*Taxidea taxus*
California Ground Squirrel	*Spermophilus beecheyi*
California Sea Lion	*Zalophus californianus*
California Vole	*Microtus californicus*
Coyote	*Canis latrans*
Killer Whale	*Orcinus orca*
Mule Deer	*Odocoileus hemionus*
Pocket Gopher	*Thomomys bottae*
Sea Otter	*Enhydra lutris*
Weasel	*Mustela frenata*
Wild Boar	*Sus scrofa*

Birds

Albatross, Black-footed	*Diomedea nigripes*
Laysan	*Diomedea immutabilis*
Short-tailed	*Diomedea albatrus*
American Avocet	*Recurvirostra americana*
American Coot	*Fulica americana*
American Robin	*Turdus migratorius*
Auklet, Cassin's	*Ptychoramphus aleuticus*
Parakeet	*Cyclorrhynchus psittacula*
Rhinoceros	*Cerorhinca monocerata*
Blackbird, Brewer's	*Euphagus cyanocephalus*
Red-winged	*Agelaius phoeniceus*
Tricolored	*Agelaius tricolor*
Black-legged Kittiwake	*Rissa tridactyla*
Black-necked Stilt	*Himantopus mexicanus*
Black Oystercatcher	*Haematopus bachmani*
Blue-gray Gnatcatcher	*Polioptila caerulea*
Brown-headed Cowbird	*Molothrus ater*
Bufflehead	*Bucephala albeola*
Bunting, Indigo	*Passerina cyanea*
Lark	*Calamospiza melanocorys*
Lazuli	*Passerina amoena*
Painted	*Passerina ciris*
Snow	*Plectrophenax nivalis*
Bushtit	*Psaltriparus minimus*

California Condor	*Gymnogyps californianus*
California Thrasher	*Toxostoma redivivum*
Chaffinch	*Fringilla coelebs*
Chickadee, Carolina	*Parus carolinensis*
Chestnut-backed	*Parus rufescens*
Chicken	*Gallus domesticus*
Clark's Nutcracker	*Nucifraga columbiana*
Common Crow	*Corvus brachyrhynchos*
Common Flicker	*Colaptes auratus*
Common Goldeneye	*Bucephala clangula*
Common Nighthawk	*Chordeiles minor*
Common Snipe	*Capella gallinago*
Common Yellowthroat	*Geothlypis trichas*
Cormorant, Brandt's	*Phalacrocorax penicillatus*
Double-crested	*Phalacrocorax auritus*
Pelagic	*Phalacrocorax pelagicus*
Dove, Inca	*Scardafella inca*
Mourning	*Zenaida macroura*
Rock ("pigeon")	*Columba livia*
White-winged	*Zenaida asiatica*
Dowitcher, Long-billed	*Limnodromus scolopaceus*
Short-billed	*Limnodromus griseus*
Dunlin	*Calidris alpina*
Eagle, Bald	*Haliaeetus leucocephalus*
Golden	*Aquila chrysaetos*
Egret, Great	*Casmerodius albus*
Snowy	*Egretta thula*
Finch, House	*Carpodacus mexicanus*
Purple	*Carpodacus purpureus*
Flycatcher, Ash-throated	*Myiarchus cinerascens*
Olive-sided	*Nuttallornis borealis*
Western	*Empidonax difficilis*
Willow	*Empidonax traillii*
Goldfinch, Lawrence's	*Carduelis lawrencei*
Lesser	*Carduelis psaltria*
Grackle, Boat-tailed	*Quiscalus major*
Common	*Quiscalus quiscula*
Great-tailed	*Quiscalus mexicanus*
Great Auk	*Pinguinis impennis*

Grebe, Eared	*Podiceps nigricollis*
Horned	*Podiceps auritus*
Pied-billed	*Podilymbus podiceps*
Red-necked	*Podiceps grisegena*
Western	*Aechmophorus occidentalis*
Grosbeak, Black-headed	*Pheucticus melanocephalus*
Blue	*Guiraca caerulea*
Grouse, Ruffed	*Bonasa umbellus*
Sage	*Centrocercus urophasianus*
Gull, Bonaparte's	*Larus philadelphia*
California	*Larus californicus*
Heermann's	*Larus heermanni*
Ring-billed	*Larus delawarensis*
Sabine's	*Xema sabini*
Western	*Larus occidentalis*
Hawk, Cooper's	*Accipiter cooperii*
Marsh	*Circus cyaneus*
Red-shouldered	*Buteo lineatus*
Red-tailed	*Buteo jamaicensis*
Sharp-shinned	*Accipiter striatus*
Heron, Black-crowned Night	*Nycticorax nycticorax*
Great Blue	*Ardea herodias*
Green	*Butorides striatus*
House Sparrow	*Passer domesticus*
Hummingbird, Allen's	*Selasphorus sasin*
Anna's	*Calypte anna*
Black-chinned	*Archilochus alexandri*
Jaeger, Parasitic	*Stercorarius parasiticus*
Pomarine	*Stercorarius pomarinus*
Jay, Scrub	*Aphelocoma coerulescens*
Steller's	*Cyanocitta stelleri*
Junco, Dark-eyed	*Junco hyemalis*
Point Pinos	*Junco hyemalis pinosus*
Lesser Scaup	*Aythya affinis*
Long-billed Curlew	*Numenius americanus*
Loon, Arctic	*Gavia arctica*
Common	*Gavia immer*
Red-throated	*Gavia stellata*
Yellow-billed	*Gavia adamsii*
Magnificent Frigate-bird	*Fregata magnificens*
Mallard	*Anas platyrhynchos*

Marbled Godwit	*Limosa fedoa*
Merlin	*Falco columbarius*
Mockingbird	*Mimus polyglottos*
Murre, Common	*Uria aalge*
Thick-billed	*Uria lomvia*
Murrelet, Ancient	*Synthliboramphus antiquus*
Craveri's	*Endomychura craveri*
Marbled	*Brachyramphus marmoratus*
Xantus'	*Endomychura hypoleuca*
Northern Fulmar	*Fulmarus glacialis*
Northern Oriole	*Icterus galbula*
Northern Pintail	*Anas acuta*
Northern Shoveler	*Anas clypeata*
Nuthatch, Pigmy	*Sitta pygmaea*
Red-breasted	*Sitta canadensis*
White-breasted	*Sitta carolinensis*
Osprey	*Pandion haliaetus*
Owl, Barn	*Tyto alba*
Burrowing	*Athene cunicularia*
Flammulated	*Otus flammeolus*
Great Horned	*Bubo virginianus*
Long-eared	*Asio otus*
Pigmy	*Glaucidium gnoma*
Saw-whet	*Aegolius acadicus*
Screech	*Otus asio*
Short-eared	*Asio flammeus*
Pelican, Brown	*Pelecanus occidentalis*
White	*Pelecanus erythrorhynchos*
Peregrine Falcon	*Falco peregrinus*
Phainopepla	*Phainopepla nitens*
Phalarope, Northern (Red-necked)	*Lobipes lobatus*
Red	*Phalaropus fulicarius*
Wilson's	*Steganopus tricolor*
Pigeon, Band-tailed	*Columba fasciata*
Passenger	*Ectopistes migratorius*
Pigeon Guillemot	*Cepphus columba*
Plain Titmouse	*Parus inornatus*
Plover, Black-bellied	*Pluvialis squatarola*
Semipalmated	*Charadrius semipalmatus*
Snowy	*Charadrius alexandrinus*
Poor-will	*Phalaenoptilus nuttallii*

Puffin, Horned	*Fratercula corniculata*
Tufted	*Lunda cirrhata*
Purple Martin	*Progne subis*
Quail, California	*Lophortyx californicus*
Mountain	*Oreortyx pictus*
Rail, California Clapper	*Rallus longirostris obsoletus*
Clapper	*Rallus longirostris*
Virginia	*Rallus limicola*
Red-breasted Merganser	*Mergus serrator*
Red Knot	*Calidris canutus*
Ruby-crowned Kinglet	*Regulus calendula*
Ruddy Duck	*Oxyura jamaicensis*
Sanderling	*Calidris alba*
Sandpiper, Baird's	*Calidris bairdii*
Least	*Calidris minutilla*
Pectoral	*Calidris melanotos*
Red-backed	*Calidris alpina*
Spotted	*Actitis macularia*
Western	*Calidris mauri*
Sapsucker, Red-breasted	*Sphyrapicus ruber*
Yellow-bellied	*Sphyrapicus varius*
Shearwater, Manx	*Puffinus puffinus*
New Zealand	*Puffinus bulleri*
Pink-footed	*Puffinus creatopus*
Short-tailed	*Puffinus tenuirostris*
(Slender-billed)	
Sooty	*Puffinus griseus*
Streaked	*Puffinus leucomelas*
Skua	*Catharacta skua*
Sora	*Porzana carolina*
Sparrow, Black-chinned	*Spizella atrogularis*
Chipping	*Spizella passerina*
Field	*Spizella pusilla*
Fox	*Passerella iliaca*
Gambel's White-	*Zonotrichia leucophrys gambelii*
crowned	
Golden-crowned	*Zonotrichia atricapilla*
Grasshopper	*Ammodramus savannarum*
Harris'	*Zonotrichia querula*
Lark	*Chondestes grammacus*

Nuttall's White-crowned	*Zonotrichia leucophrys nuttalli*
Puget Sound White-crowned	*Zonotrichia leucophrys pugetensis*
Rufous-crowned	*Aimophila ruficeps*
Sage	*Amphispiza belli*
Savannah	*Passerculus sandwichensis*
Song	*Melospiza melodia*
Swamp	*Melospiza georgiana*
Vesper	*Pooecetes gramineus*
White-crowned	*Zonotrichia leucophrys*
White-throated	*Zonotrichia albicollis*
Starling	*Sturnus vulgaris*
Storm-petrel, Ashy	*Oceanodroma homochroa*
Black	*Oceanodroma melania*
Fork-tailed	*Oceanodroma furcata*
Galapagos	*Oceanodroma tethys*
Leach's	*Oceanodroma leucorhoa*
Least	*Halocyptena microsoma*
Surfbird	*Aphriza virgata*
Surf Scoter	*Melanitta perspicillata*
Swallow, Bank	*Riparia riparia*
Barn	*Hirundo rustica*
Cliff	*Petrochelidon pyrrhonota*
Rough-winged	*Stelgidopteryx ruficollis*
Tree	*Iridoprocne bicolor*
Violet-green	*Tachycineta thalassina*
Swift, Black	*Cypseloides niger*
Vaux's	*Chaetura vauxi*
White-throated	*Aeronautes saxatalis*
Teal, Cinnamon	*Anas cyanoptera*
Green-winged	*Anas crecca*
Tern, Caspian	*Sterna caspia*
Elegant	*Sterna elegans*
Forster's	*Sterna forsteri*
Least	*Sterna albifrons*
Royal	*Sterna maxima*
Thrush, Hermit	*Catharus guttatus*
Swainson's	*Catharus ustulatus*
Towhee, Brown	*Pipilo fuscus*
Rufous-sided	*Pipilo erythrophthalmus*

Turkey Vulture	*Cathartes aura*
Turnstone, Black	*Arenaria melanocephala*
Ruddy	*Arenaria interpres*
Verdin	*Auriparus flaviceps*
Vireo, Bell's	*Vireo bellii*
Hutton's	*Vireo huttoni*
Solitary	*Vireo solitarius*
Warbling	*Vireo gilvus*
Wandering Tattler	*Heteroscelus incanus*
Warbler, Black-throated Gray	*Dendroica nigrescens*
Golden-cheeked	*Dendroica chrysoparia*
Kirtland's	*Dendroica kirtlandii*
MacGillivray's	*Oporornis tolmiei*
Orange-crowned	*Vermivora celata*
Parula	*Parula americana*
Wilson's	*Wilsonia pusilla*
Yellow	*Dendroica petechia*
Yellow-rumped	*Dendroica coronata*
Western Kingbird	*Tyrannus verticalis*
Western Wood Pewee	*Contopus sordidulus*
Whimbrel	*Numenius phaeopus*
White-faced Ibis	*Plegadis chihi*
White-tailed Kite	*Elanus leucurus*
Willet	*Catoptrophorus semipalmatus*
Woodpecker, Acorn	*Melanerpes formicivorus*
Downy	*Picoides pubescens*
Hairy	*Picoides villosus*
Nuttall's	*Picoides nuttallii*
Wren, Bewick's	*Thryomanes bewickii*
House	*Troglodytes aedon*
Long-billed Marsh	*Cistothorus palustris*
Winter	*Troglodytes troglodytes*
Wrentit	*Chamaea fasciata*
Yellow-billed Magpie	*Pica nuttalli*
Yellow-breasted Chat	*Icteria virens*
Yellowlegs, Greater	*Tringa melanoleuca*
Lesser	*Tringa flavipes*

Common and Scientific Names for Fishes

Fishes

Arrow Goby	*Clevelandia ios*
Blenny	*Hypsoblennius* sp.
Bonito	*Sarda chiliensis*
Grunion	*Leuresthes tenuis*
Northern Anchovy	*Engraulis mordax*
Pacific Sardine	*Sardinops sagax*
Sand Dab	*Citharichthys* sp.
Sculpin	Cottidae
Shiner Perch	*Cymatogaster aggregata*

Common and Scientific Names for Invertebrates

Invertebrates

Abalone	*Haliotis* sp.
Beach Hopper	*Orchestoidea* sp.
Brine Fly	*Ephydra gracilis*
Brine Shrimp	*Artemia salina*
Ghost Shrimp	*Callianassa californiensis*
Grasshopper	*Melanoplus* sp.
Horse Mussel	*Volsella modiolus*
Krill	Euphausiacea
Limpet	*Acmaea* sp.
Lined Shore Crab	*Pachygrapsus crassipes*
Market Squid	*Loligo opalescens*
Mormon Cricket	*Anabrus simplex*
Mud Crab	*Hemigrapsus oregonensis*
Mud Shrimp	*Upogebia pugettensis*
Mussel	*Mytilus* sp.
Ochre Star	*Pisaster ochraceus*
Owl Limpet	*Lottia gigantea*
Periwinkle	*Littorina* sp.
Sand Crab	*Emerita analoga*
Sand Flea	*Orchestoidea* sp.
Shore Fly	*Ephydra gracilis*
Water Boatman	*Trichocorixa reticulata*
Yellow Shore Crab	*Hemigrapsus oregonensis*

Common and Scientific Names for Plants

Plants

Alder, Red	*Alnus rubra*
White	*Alnus rhombifolia*
Barley	*Hordeum* sp.
Bigleaf Maple	*Acer macrophyllum*
Black Cottonwood	*Populus trichocarpa*
Black Sage	*Salvia mellifera*
Bluegrass	*Poa* sp.
Bracken	*Pteridium aquilinum*
Brass Buttons	*Cotula coronopifolia*
Bromegrass	*Bromus* sp.
Broomcorn Millet	*Panicum miliaceum*
Bulrush	*Scirpus* sp.
California Boxelder	*Acer negundo* ssp. *californicum*
California Laurel	*Umbellularia californica*
California Sagebrush	*Artemisia californica*
California Sycamore	*Platanus racemosa*
California Tule	*Scirpus californicus*
California Wild Rose	*Rosa californica*
Cat-tail, Broad-leaved	*Typha latifolia*
Narrow-leaved	*Typha augustifolia*
Ceanothus	*Ceanothus* sp.
Chamise	*Adenostoma fasciculatum*
Coffeeberry	*Rhamnus californica*
Cordgrass	*Spartina foliosa*
Coyote Brush	*Baccharis pilularis* ssp. *consanguinea*
Cream Bush	*Holodiscus discolor*
Currant	*Ribes* sp.
Cypress, Gowen	*Cupressus goveniana*
Monterey	*Cupressus macrocarpa*
Darnel	*Lolium* sp.
Duckweed	*Lemna* sp.
Eel-grass	*Zostera marina*
Fescue, Annual (introduced)	*Vulpia* sp.
Perennial (native)	*Festuca* sp.
Fir, Douglas	*Pseudotsuga menziesii*
Bristlecone (Santa Lucia)	*Abies bracteata*

Fleshy Jaumea	*Jaumea carnosa*
Giraffe Head	*Lamium amplexicaule*
Gooseberry	*Ribes* sp.
Hollyleaf Redberry	*Rhamnus ilicifolia*
Huckleberry	*Vaccinium* sp.
Kelp, Bull	*Nereocystis luetkeana*
Giant	*Macrocystis* sp.
Madrone	*Arbutus menziesii*
Manzanita	*Arctostaphylos* sp.
Melic Grass	*Melica* sp.
Mistletoe	*Phoradendron* sp.
Needlegrass	*Stipa* sp.
Oak, Black	*Quercus kelloggii*
Blue	*Quercus douglasii*
Canyon Live	*Quercus chrysolepis*
Coast Live	*Quercus agrifolia*
Interior Live	*Quercus wislizenii*
Valley	*Quercus lobata*
Oat	*Avena* sp.
Pacific Blackberry	*Rubus ursinus*
Pickleweed	*Salicornia virginica*
Pine, Bishop	*Pinus muricata*
Coulter	*Pinus coulteri*
Digger	*Pinus sabiniana*
Monterey	*Pinus radiata*
Poison-oak	*Toxicodendron diversiloba*
Purple Needlegrass	*Stipa pulchra*
Redwood	*Sequoia sempervirens*
Rushes	*Juncus* sp.
Ryegrass (introduced)	*Lolium* sp.
Ryegrass (native)	*Elymus* sp.
Salal	*Gaultheria shallon*
Saltgrass	*Distichlis spicata* var. *spicata*
Sedges	*Carex* sp.
Silver Hairgrass	*Aira caryophyllea*
Silverweed	*Potentilla egedii*
Snowberry	*Symphoricarpos rivularis*
Spike Rush	*Eleocharis* sp.
Spreading Snowberry	*Symphoricarpos mollis*
Squirrel-tail	*Sitanion jubatum*

Sticky Monkey-flower,	
Northern	*Mimulus aurantiacus*
Santa Lucia	*Mimulus bifidus* ssp. *fasciculatus*
Tanoak	*Lithocarpus densiflorus*
Thimbleberry	*Rubus parviflorus* var. *velutinus*
Three Square	*Scirpus americanus*
Toyon	*Heteromeles arbutifolia*
Western Creek Dogwood	*Cornus occidentalis*
Wigeon Grass	*Ruppia maritima*
Wild Lilac	*Ceanothus* sp.
Willow, Arroyo	*Salix lasiolepis*
Red	*Salix laevigata*
Sandbar	*Salix hindsiana*
Wire Grass	*Eleocharis macrostachya*

APPENDIX B

LIST OF THE BIRDS OF THE MONTEREY PENINSULA REGION
Monterey County, California

published by
THE MONTEREY PENINSULA AUDUBON SOCIETY
Carmel, California

Sixth edition revised June 15, 1977

Compiled by the Check-List Committee

Copyright 1977

by

Monterey Peninsula Audubon Society

Box 5656, Carmel, California 93921

Price: 10¢ each

For mail orders send
stamped self-addressed business envelope.

Area covered: The entire Monterey Peninsula region including all points within a 7.5 mile radius of Jacks Peak, plus the waters of Monterey Bay and the Pacific Ocean adjacent to the Peninsula. The landward boundary approximates an arc from the Main Garrison Gate of Fort Ord through the Los Laureles Road of Carmel Valley to Malpaso Creek, the southern limit. **Names** used and the order in which they appear are those in the fifth edition of the American Ornithologists Union Check-list of North American Birds (1957) and the 32nd and 33rd Supplements published in *The Auk.*

ABBREVIATIONS (See also note below on SCARCITY-ABUNDANCE DESIGNATIONS).

A—**Abundant:** greatest relative numbers.

acc.—**Accidental:** definitely recorded more than once but **never more than a few times,** nor with any regularity (see R—**Rare** below).

aer.—**Aerial:** seen in flight over almost any habitat. However, one or more usual habitats may also be indicated by a number (see **NUMERALS** below).

C—**Common:** next below A (abundant) in relative numbers.

e—**Edge:** found on edge of indicated habitat and not usually in its midst, e.g., the Brewer's Blackbird, which is not found in continuous forest growths, will nest on edges of stands of pines and oaks (10e,11e), or where such trees grow singly or in groups with open areas in between.

F—**Fall:** any period from the end of July until the end of November.

f.c.—**Fairly common:** next below C (common) in relative numbers.

irr.—**Irregular:** present in numbers which vary from year to year (compare with spor.—**Sporadic**).

L—**Local:** found only at certain particular places.

O—**Offshore species:** can usually be observed only from a boat on Monterey Bay or the Pacific. However, some of these have been seen from shore.

P—**Permanent Resident:** the species but not necessarily the individual remains the year around.

R—**Rare:** lowest relative numbers, but still regular in occurrence.

recs.—**Records:** used in parentheses to indicate that there also have been some records of occurrence at another season.

S—**Summer Visitant:** some summer visitants arrive as early as February; some may remain until October.

spor.—**Sporadic:** some years present, some years absent; in some cases many years of absence may intervene between occurrences.

Spr.—**Spring:** any period from February through May.

T—**Transient:** migrant, usually occurring in both spring and fall. (See definitions for Spr. and F).

U—**Uncommon:** next above R (rare) in relative numbers.

vic.—**In vicinity,** i.e., other parts of Monterey County, but not within the limits of the area covered.

W—**Winter Visitant:** some winter visitants may arrive as early as August; some may remain as late as May.

NOTE: SCARCITY-ABUNDANCE DESIGNATIONS are not offered as absolute numerical classifications, but rather for the purpose of generalized quantitative comparisons (a) between related species, or (b) between unrelated species in the same habitat, or (c) between differing seasonal status, where such occurs, within the same species. These designations are graded upwards as follows: **single occurrence** (along with birds which are not part of the expected avifauna of our region) these appear on List No. 2 (Supplementary List) only; **acc.; R; U; f.c.; C; A.**

NUMERALS refer to habitats, as follows:
1. Ocean and bays within binocular range from shore. (Compare "O" — offshore species.)
2. Rocky shore.
3. Beaches, sand bars, mudflats.
4. Lagoons, ponds, larger streams.
5. Marshes (wet grass areas) and/or tule-cattail swamps.
6. Open fields and/or golf courses.
7. Low brush in general and/or chaparral of dry hillsides.
8. Tall brush in general and/or timber of shaded hillsides and canyons.
9. Stream bottom thickets and/or river bottom deciduous woodland.
10. Oak groves, or oak woodland.
11. Pine and cypress woodlands.
12. Gardens, planted areas, buildings, and village streets.

Numerals within parentheses—( )—indicate a less usual habitat.
Numerals followed by an "e" indicate the "edge" of a habitat. See "e" in list of abbreviations.

LIST NO. 1 (Regularly Occurring Birds)

LOONS
............**Common Loon**—CW:1,(4) ....
............**Yellow-billed Loon**—acc.W:1 ....
............**Arctic (Pacific) Loon**—CW,AT:1(4) ....
............**Red-throated Loon**—f.c.W:1,4 ....

GREBES
............**Red-necked Grebe**—UW:1 ....
............**Horned Grebe**—CW:1,4 ....
............**Eared Grebe**—CW:1,4 ....
............**Western Grebe**—AW:1,4 ....
............**Pied-billed Grebe**—P(AW,LS):4(1) ....

............**BLACK-FOOTED ALBATROSS**—OP(CS,RW) ....

SHEARWATERS, FULMARS
............**Northern Fulmar**—Oirr. W.(RS) ....
............**Pink-footed Shearwater**—OP(CS,RW) ....
............**Flesh-footed (Pale-footed) Shearwater**—OR ....
............**New Zealand Shearwater**—ORF ....
............**Sooty Shearwater**—OP(AT,AS,RW):1 ....
............**Short-tailed (Slender-billed) Shearwater**—Oirr.F(Spr.recs.) ....
............**Manx (Black-vented) Shearwater**—Ospor.F:1 ....

STORM-PETRELS
............**Fork-tailed Storm-Petrel**—Ospor. ....
............**Leach's Storm-Petrel**—Ospor.F ....
............**Ashy Storm-Petrel**—OCS(Wrecs.)(1) ....
............**Black Storm-Petrel**—Of.c.F(1) ....
............**Wilson's Storm-Petrel**—ORF ....

PELICANS
.... **White Pelican**—acc.(spor.vic.) ....
.... **Brown Pelican**—CP:1,2,4 ....

CORMORANTS
.... **Double-crested Cormorant**—RW,UT:1,2,4 ....
.... **Brandt's Cormorant**—AP:1,2 ....
.... **Pelagic Cormorant**—CP:1,2 ....

HERONS, EGRETS, BITTERNS
.... **Great Blue Heron**—f.c.P:4,5(1,2,6) ....
.... **Green Heron**—f.c.S(RW):4(2,5) ....
.... **Cattle Egret**—spor.W:6 ....
.... **Great (Common) Egret**—RW:4,5(1) ....
.... **Snowy Egret**—RW:4,5 ....
.... **Black-crowned Night Heron**—CP:2,4,5 ....
.... **American Bittern**—RW:5 ....

.... **WHISTLING SWAN**—acc.W:4 ....

GEESE
.... **Canada Goose**—RW:4,5(6) ....
.... **Brant**—UW,f.c.T:1(6) ....
.... **White-fronted Goose**—RW ....
.... **Snow Goose**—RW ....
.... **Ross' Goose**—acc.W ....

DUCKS
.... **Mallard**—AW(LS):4,5 ....
.... **Gadwall**—RW:4,5 ....
.... **Pintail**—AW:4,5 ....
.... **Green-winged Teal**—f.c.W:4,5 ....
.... **Blue-winged Teal**—acc.W ....
.... **Cinnamon Teal**—UW,LS:4,5 ....
.... **European Wigeon**—acc.W ....
.... **American Wigeon (Baldpate)**—CW:4,5 ....
.... **Northern Shoveler**—AW:4,5 ....
.... **Wood Duck**—RW:4(S vic.) ....
.... **Redhead**—RW:4,5 ....
.... **Ring-necked Duck**—RW:4 ....
.... **Canvasback**—CW:4 ....
.... **Greater Scaup**—RW:1,4 ....
.... **Lesser Scaup**—CW:1,4 ....
.... **Common (American) Golden-eye**—f.c.W:1,4 ....
.... **Bufflehead**—CW:4 ....
.... **Oldsquaw**—RW:1 ....
.... **Harlequin Duck**—acc.W(S.recs.) ....
.... **White-winged Scoter**—P(CW,US):1,(4) ....
.... **Surf Scoter**—P(AW,US):1,(4) ....
.... **Black (Common) Scoter**—RW:1 ....
.... **Ruddy Duck**—AP(LS):4 ....
.... **Hooded Merganser**—acc.W ....
.... **Common Merganser**—RW:4(S.vic.) ....
.... **Red-breasted Merganser**—CW:1,4 ....

.... **TURKEY VULTURE**—P(CS,RW)aer. ....

KITES, HAWKS, EAGLES, OSPREY
.... **White-tailed Kite**—Rspor.P:5,6,9,10e ....
.... **Sharp-shinned Hawk**—UP:8-11 ....
.... **Cooper's Hawk**—f.c.P:8-11 ....
.... **Red-tailed Hawk**—CP:aer,6 ....
.... **Red-shouldered Hawk**—UP:9,10 ....
.... **Golden Eagle**—RP:aer,6 ....
.... **Bald Eagle**—acc.W ....
.... **Marsh Hawk**—RW:5,6 ....
.... **Osprey**—acc.T ....

FALCONS: DUCK, PIGEON and SPARROW HAWKS
.... **Prairie Falcon**—acc.(Pvic.) ....
.... **Peregrine Falcon**—RW:aer.,1,5 ....
.... **Merlin (Pigeon Hawk)**—acc.W ....
.... **American Kestrel (Sparrow Hawk)**—CP:6,7e-11e,12 ....

QUAIL
.... **California Quail**—AP:6e,7,8e-10e,12 ....
.... **Mountain Quail**—RS(Cvic.):8 ....

RAILS, GALLINULES, COOTS
.... **Clapper Rail**—acc.(Pvic.) ....
.... **Virginia Rail**—f.c.W:5
.... **Sora**—f.c.W:5 ....
.... **Common Gallinule**—RW:4,5 ....
.... **Coot**—P(AW,LS):4,5 ....

.... **BLACK OYSTERCATCHER**—CP:2 ....

PLOVERS, SURFBIRDS, TURNSTONES
.... **Semipalmated Plover**—CT:3 ....
.... **Snowy Plover**—f.c.W:3(Svic.) ....
.... **Killdeer**—CP:3,5,6 ....
.... **American Golden Plover**—RT:3 ....
.... **Black-bellied Plover**—f.c.W:3 ....
.... **Surfbird**—f.c.W:2 ....
.... **Ruddy Turnstone**—UTW:2,3 ....
.... **Black Turnstone**—AW:2,3 ....

SNIPES, SANDPIPERS, CURLEWS, GODWITS, etc.
.... **Common (Wilson's) Snipe**—CW:5 ....
.... **Long-billed Curlew**—UT,RW:3(5,6) ....
.... **Whimbrel (Hudsonian Curlew)**—CT,RW:3(5,6) ....
.... **Spotted Sandpiper**—RW:2(3) ....
.... **Solitary Sandpiper**—acc. ....
.... **Wandering Tattler**—CT,RW:2 ....
.... **Willet**—P(CW,US):3(5) ....
.... **Greater Yellowlegs**—f.c.T,RW:3,5 ....
.... **Lesser Yellowlegs**—RF:3,5 ....
.... **Red Knot**—acc. ....
.... **Rock Sandpiper**—acc. ....
.... **Pectoral Sandpiper**—RF:3,5 ....
.... **Baird's Sandpiper**—RF:3 ....
.... **Least Sandpiper**—AT,f.c.W:3,5 ....
.... **Dunlin**—UT,RW:3 ....
.... **Short-billed Dowitcher**—CT,RW:3(5) ....
.... **Long-billed Dowitcher**—CT:3(5) ....
.... **Western Sandpiper**—AT:3 ....
.... **Marbled Godwit**—CT,UW:3 ....
.... **Sanderling**—AW:3 ....

.... **AMERICAN AVOCET**—RT:3,4(P.vic.) ....

.... **BLACK-NECKED STILT**—acc.(S.vic.) ....

PHALAROPES
.... **Red Phalarope**—AT,spor.W:1,4 ....
.... **Wilson's Phalarope**—RT:4 ....
.... **Northern Phalarope**—AT:1,4 ....

JAEGERS, SKUAS
.... **Pomarine Jaeger**—O(CF,RW) ....
.... **Parasitic Jaeger**—OCT(S&W recs.) ....
.... **Long-tailed Jaeger**—acc. ....
.... **Skua**—OR

GULLS
.... **Glaucous Gull**—RW:1,2,3 ....
.... **Glaucous-winged Gull**—AW:1-4(6) ....
.... **Western Gull**—AP:1-4(6) ....
.... **Herring Gull**—CW:1-4(6) ....
.... **Thayer's Gull**—RW:1-4(6) ....
.... **California Gull**—AW:1-4(6) ....
.... **Ring-billed Gull**—UW:3,4(1,6) ....
.... **Mew (Short-billed) Gull**—AW:1-4(6) ....
.... **Bonaparte's Gull**—irr.T,RW:1,3,4 ....
.... **Heermann's Gull**—P(AF,CW,RSpr.CS)1-4 ....
.... **Black-legged Kittiwake**—irr.W(S recs.):1,2 ....
.... **Sabine's Gull**—O.f.c.T. ....

TERNS

.... **Forster's Tern**—T(P.vic.)
.... **Common Tern**—T.
.... **Arctic Tern**—T(F only?)
.... **Least Tern**—acc.
.... **Elegant Tern**—irr.F:1
.... **Caspian Tern**—UT:3,4
.... **Black Tern**—acc.

ALCIDS: AUKS, MURRES, PUFFINS, etc.

.... **Common Murre**—P(AW):1
.... **Thick-billed Murre**—acc.W:1
.... **Pigeon Guillemot**—P(CLS,UW):1,2
.... **Marbled Murrelet**—RW:1
.... **Xantus' Murrelet**—ORF
.... **Craveri's Murrelet**—Oacc.F
.... **Ancient Murrelet**—UW:1
.... **Cassin's Auklet**—CW:1(OAF&W,S recs.)
.... **Rhinoceros Auklet**—AW:1
.... **Tufted Puffin**—OR

PIGEONS, DOVES

.... **Band-tailed Pigeon**—P(CW,LS):6,8,10-12
.... **Mourning Dove**—CP:6,9e

.... **ROADRUNNER**—RLP:7

OWLS

.... **Barn Owl**—f.c.P:aer.,6,12
.... **Screech Owl**—f.c.P:10(8,9,12)
.... **Great Horned Owl**—CP:8,11
.... **Pygmy Owl**—f.c.P:8,11
.... **Burrowing Owl**—RW:6
.... **Spotted Owl**—RP:8
.... **Long-eared Owl**—acc.(P.vic.)
.... **Short-eared Owl**—acc.(W.vic.)
.... **Saw-whet Owl**—RP:8,11

.... **POOR-WILL**—RP:7(CSvic.)

SWIFTS

.... **Black Swift**—RT:aer.,2(Svic.)
.... **Vaux's Swift**—RT:aer.
.... **White-throated Swift**—P(UW,AS):aer.,2

HUMMINGBIRDS

.... **Black-chinned Hummingbird**—acc.(S.vic.)
.... **Costa's Hummingbird**—acc.(S.vic.)
.... **Anna's Hummingbird**—AP:7-12
.... **Rufous Hummingbird**—f.c.T:7-12
.... **Allen's Hummingbird**—AS:7-12
.... **Calliope Hummingbird**—RT

.... **BELTED KINGFISHER**—f.c.P:2,4

WOODPECKERS, FLICKERS, SAPSUCKERS

.... **Common (Red-shafted) Flicker**—AP:6e,7e,8-12
.... **Acorn Woodpecker**—AP:10,12
.... **Lewis' Woodpecker**—spor.W
.... **Yellow-bellied Sapsucker**—UW:8-10,12
.... **Hairy Woodpecker**—CP:8,9,11
.... **Downy Woodpecker**—CP:9,(8,10)
.... **Nuttall's Woodpecker**—UP:8,9,10

FLYCATCHERS, KINGBIRDS, PHOEBES

.... **Tropical Kingbird**—RFT:6(Wrecs.)
.... **Western Kingbird**—acc.(S.vic.)
.... **Cassin's Kingbird**—acc.(S.vic.)
.... **Ash-throated Flycatcher**—RT:7,8(S.vic)
.... **Black Phoebe**—AP:4e,5e,6e,9e,12(2e,3e,8e,10e)
.... **Say's Phoebe**—CW:6(3e)7e(S.vic)
.... **Willow (Traill's) Flycatcher**—acc.
.... **Western Flycatcher**—AS:8,9,11,12(10)

.... **Western Wood Pewee**—US:9(CSvic.) ....
.... **Olive-sided Flycatcher**—CS:8,11(9e) ....

.... **HORNED LARK**—P(f.c.W,LS):6 ....

SWALLOWS, MARTINS
.... **Violet-green Swallow**—P(AS,spor.W):aer,4-6,10e,11e
.... **Tree Swallow**—P(CS,spor.W):aer.,4-6 ....
.... **Bank Swallow**—acc.(LS vic.)
.... **Rough-winged Swallow**—CS:aer,4-6
.... **Barn Swallow**—CS:aer.,4-6,12
.... **Cliff Swallow**—AS:aer.,4-6,12
.... **Purple Martin**—RT,LS:aer.,9e

JAYS, MAGPIES, CROWS, NUTCRACKERS
.... **Steller's Jay**—CP:11 ....
.... **Scrub Jay**—AP:7-10,12
.... **Yellow-billed Magpie**—LP:6,10e,12
.... **Common Raven**—acc.(Pvic.)
.... **Common Crow**—AP:3e,6,8,10,12
.... **Clark's Nutcracker**—spor.W

TITMICE, CHICKADEES, BUSHTITS
.... **Chestnut-backed Chickadee**—AP:8-12
.... **Plain Titmouse**—CP:10,12
.... **Bushtit**—AP:7-10,11e,12 ....

NUTHATCHES
.... **White-breasted Nuthatch**—RLP:10 (CP vic.) ....
.... **Red-breasted Nuthatch**—spor.W.(S.vic.) ....
.... **Pygmy Nuthatch**—AP:11,12 ....

.... **BROWN CREEPER**—CP:8,11 ....

.... **WRENTIT**—AP:7-9 ....

WRENS
.... **House Wren**—P(RW,US):7-10,12 ....
.... **Winter Wren**—P(CW,RLS):8,9,11
.... **Bewick's Wren**—AP:7-9,11e,12 ....
.... **Long-billed Marsh Wren**—CW(LS?):5 ....
.... **Canyon Wren**—RLP
.... **Rock Wren**—acc.(P.vic.) ....

MOCKINGBIRDS, THRASHERS
.... **Mockingbird**—CP:7,12
.... **California Thrasher**—UP:7,8,9e,12 ....

THRUSHES, ROBINS, BLUEBIRDS, SOLITAIRES
.... **American Robin**—P(AW,CS)6,8-12 ....
.... **Varied Thrush**—irr.W:8,11,12 ....
.... **Hermit Thrush**—P(AW:8-12,US:11) ....
.... **Swainson's Thrush**—AS:9(12) ....
.... **Western Bluebird**—P(f.c.W,LS):6,9e,10e,11e,12 ....
.... **Townsend's Solitaire**—acc.W.

GNATCATCHERS, KINGLETS
.... **Blue-gray Gnatcatcher**—RW:7 (S.vic.) ....
.... **Golden-crowned Kinglet**—irr.W:11
.... **Ruby-crowned Kinglet**—AW:8-12 ....

.... **WATER PIPIT**—CW:3e,5e,6 ....

.... **CEDAR WAXWING**—irr.W:12 ....

.... **LOGGERHEAD SHRIKE**—f.c.W:6 ....

.... **STARLING**—AP:6,12(2) ....

VIREOS
.... **Hutton's Vireo**—CP:8-12 ....
.... **Solitary Vireo**—RT:8,9(CSvic.) ....
.... **Warbling Vireo**—AS:9,(10,12) ....

WOOD WARBLERS, YELLOWTHROAT, CHAT
.... Black-and-white Warbler—RTF:9,11,12 ....
.... Tennessee Warbler—RTF:11,12 ....
.... Orange-crowned Warbler—P(UW,AS):8,9,12,(10) ....
.... Nashville Warbler—RT:9(11,12) ....
.... Yellow Warbler—AS:9
.... Yellow-rumped (Audubon/Myrtle) Warbler—AW:6e,8-12(2e,3e)(S.vic.) ....
.... Black-throated Gray Warbler—RT(LS):8,10(AS vic.) ....
.... Townsend's Warbler—CW:11,12 ....
.... Hermit Warbler—RW:11
.... Blackpoll Warbler—UTF:11 ....
.... Palm Warbler—RT:9,11 ....
.... Northern Waterthrush—RTF:9 ....
.... Macgillivray's Warbler—RT,RLS:9 ....
.... Common Yellowthroat—f.c.P:5,9e ....
.... Yellow-breasted Chat—RS:7e,9e ....
.... Wilson's Warbler—AS:9,(8) ....
.... American Redstart—RT:11,12 ....

.... HOUSE SPARROW—AP:12 ....

MEADOWLARKS, BLACKBIRDS, ORIOLES, COWBIRDS
.... Bobolink—RTF:5 ....
.... Western Meadowlark—AP:5e,6 ....
.... Yellow-headed Blackbird—acc.
.... Red-winged Blackbird—AP:5,6,(12)
.... Tricolored Blackbird—CW:5,6(Svic.) ....
.... Hooded Oriole—RLS:12
.... Northern (Bullock's/Baltimore) Oriole—RT,RLS:12(CS vic.) ....
.... Brewer's Blackbird—AP:5,6,10e,11e,12(2e,3e) ....
.... Brown-headed Cowbird—f.c.S(RW):6,9,(12) ....

.... WESTERN TANAGER—irr.T:8,11,12 (S.vic) ....

GROSBEAKS, FINCHES, SPARROWS, BUNTINGS, etc.
.... Black-headed Grosbeak—CS:9(12) ....
.... Lazuli Bunting—CS:7e ....
.... Evening Grosbeak—spor W
.... Purple Finch—CP:8e,9e,10e,11,12 ....
.... House Finch—AP:6,7e,9e,10e,12 ....
.... Pine Siskin—irr.P:6e,7e,9e,11,12 ....
.... American (Common) Goldfinch—f.c.P:6e,7e,8e,9,12 ....
.... Lesser (Green-backed) Goldfinch—AP:6e,7e,9e,11e,12 ....
.... Lawrence's Goldfinch—irr.P:6e,7e,10,11e,12 ....
.... Red Crossbill—spor.W:11 ....
.... Rufous-sided Towhee—CS:7,8,9e,12 ....
.... Brown Towhee—CP:7,9e,12 ....
.... Savannah Sparrow—P(CW,LS):5e,6 ....
.... Grasshopper Sparrow—RLS(or P?):6 ....
.... Lark Sparrow—RLP:6,7e(CP vic.) ....
.... Rufous-crowned Sparrow—ULP:7 ....
.... Sage Sparrow—RLP:7 ....
.... Dark-eyed (Slate-colored/Oregon) Junco—AP:8,11,12 ....
.... Chipping Sparrow—LS:10,11e(Wrecs.) ....
.... Black-chinned Sparrow—RLS:7 ....
.... White-crowned Sparrow—AP:6e,7,9e,12 ....
.... Golden-crowned Sparrow—AW:7-9,11e,12 ....
.... White-throated Sparrow—RW:12 ....
.... Fox Sparrow—CW:8,9,12 ....
.... Lincoln's Sparrow—UW:5e,6e,7e ....
.... Song Sparrow—CP:5,9,12 ....

LIST No. 2 (Supplementary List). The species listed below are not part of the expected avifauna of our region, but have been recorded one or more times. With more field work, it may be found that some belong in the Main List. Species indicated by * have been recorded more than once. Those marked # have been corroborated with a specimen.

Short-tailed Albatross
Laysan Albatross
Cape Petrel#
Streaked Shearwater#
Black-tailed Shearwater#
Galapagos Storm-petrel#
Least Storm-petrel*
Red-billed Tropicbird*
Blue-footed Booby
Magnificent Frigatebird*
Least Bittern*
White-faced Ibis*
Emperor Goose
Fulvous Whistling-Duck (Tree Duck)
King Eider*
California Condor#*
Broad-winged Hawk*
Swainson's Hawk
Rough-legged Hawk*
Ferruginous Hawk*
Caracara
Sandhill Crane*
Yellow Rail
Black Rail#
American Oystercatcher
Semipalmated Sandpiper*
Ruff*
Laughing Gull
Franklin's Gull*
Royal Tern
Black Skimmer
Parakeet Auklet#*
Horned Puffin#*
White-winged Dove*
Ground Dove#*
Chimney Swift
Broad-billed Hummingbird
Eastern Kingbird*
Olivaceous Flycatcher
Eastern Phoebe#*
Coues' Flycatcher
Pinyon Jay*
Gray Catbird*

Brown Thrasher*
Sage Thrasher*
Mountain Bluebird*
Bohemian Waxwing
Bell's Vireo*
Red-eyed Vireo*
Worm-eating Warbler#*
Virginia's Warbler*
Lucy's Warbler*
Northern Parula*
Magnolia Warbler#*
Cape May Warbler*
Black-throated Blue Warbler#*
Black-throated Green Warbler
Blackburnian Warbler*
Yellow-throated Warbler
Chestnut-sided Warbler*
Bay-breasted Warbler
Prairie Warbler*
Ovenbird#*
Connecticut Warbler
Hooded Warbler*
Canada Warbler*
Orchard Oriole*
Scott's Oriole
Rusty Blackbird*
Hepatic Tanager
Summer Tanager*
Rose-breasted Grosbeak#*
Indigo Bunting#*
Dickcissel
Green-tailed Towhee*
Le Conte's Sparrow
Sharp-tailed Sparrow
Vesper Sparrow*
Black-throated Sparrow
Tree Sparrow#*
Clay-colored Sparrow*
Brewer's Sparrow
Harris's Sparrow*
Swamp Sparrow*
Lapland Longspur*

LIST No. 3 Monterey County. The following additional species (omitting introduced species) have been recorded in Monterey County but not on the Peninsula. Those designated + are not considered part of the expected avifauna.

Reddish Egret+
Wood Stork+
Mountain Plover
Buff-breasted Sandpiper+
Little Gull₁+
Yellow-billed Cuckoo
Flammulated Owl
Snowy Owl#+
Lesser Nighthawk

Williamson's Sapsucker+
Dusky Flycatcher
Mountain Chickadee+
Dipper
Phainopepla
Prothonotary Warbler+
Blue Grosbeak+
Cassin's Finch
Gray-headed Junco+

INDEX

A

Acorns, as food, 94, 96
destruction of, 94-96
Acorn Woodpecker, 96-97
Activity orientation cage,
photograph, 70
Albumin, 24
Altricial, 56
American Avocet, 134-135
Annual cycle, 2, 19
Anterior pituitary, 26
Anthropomorphism, 31
AOU Check-list Committee, 5, 14

Beaches, 141-144
Shorebird species of, 143
Beck, Rollo H., 163, 184
Beechey, Frederick William, 181
Biological species concept, 7
Bird diversity,
in cemeteries, 86
in Chicago, 86
in city parks, 85
in St. Petersburg, 84
in Tucson, 85
Black, Bob, 109
Black-footed Albatross,
photograph of, 160
Black-necked Stilt, 134-135
Black Oystercatcher, 145-146
photograph of, 147
Black Swift,
discovery of nest and egg, 155, 186
nest requirements of, 156
Black Turnstone, 147-148
Branson, Ron, 108, 109
Breeding bird lists,
closed-cone coniferous
woodland, 104
freshwater areas, 128
grassland, 119
mixed evergreen forest, 108
oak (foothill) woodland, 98-99
redwood forest, 106
riparian woodland, 101
scrub, 111
Breeding seasons, equatorial, 30

Brood parasites, 50
Brood patch, 29, 53
Brown-headed cowbird, 50-52
Brown Pelican,
effect of DDT on eggs of, 154
northernmost breeding of, 154
Burrowing Owl, nesting of, 122

C

California birds,
early illustrations of, 180-181
California Clapper Rail, 137-138
California Condor, original
description of, 181
California Quail,
early illustration of, 180
original description of, 181
California Thrasher,
pair formation, 42
wing/tail ratio, 114
Caspian Tern, 136
Cassin's Auklet,
photography of, 163
Chamise, 110-111
photograph of, 112
Chaparral, 110
Christmas Bird Count, 1
Clutch size, 49-50
Coastal closed-cone coniferous
woodland, 101-104
former distribution of, 103-104
photograph of, 102
Coastal Scrub, 110-111
photograph of, 113
Coffeeberry, as food, 111
Collie, Alexander, 181
Color change without molt, 63
Common Loon, photograph of, 159
Common Murre, 154
Communities,
botanical concept of, 89
ecological concept of, 90
Courtship, 40-42
Cycle, annual, 2

D

Davidson Current Period, 158
Daylength cycle, 25
Degree of difference, 7